Macmillan Natural and Social SCIENCE

Primary 4 Pupil's Book

Pupils are reminded that they should not write in this book.

Helen Sanderson

Course consultant: Rocío Gutiérrez Burgos
Science consultant: Graham Peacock

MACMILLAN

Contents

	Content	Let's investigate!

What we already know

	Content	Let's investigate!
Unit 1 **Food and nutrition**	• Classifying food • Nutrients • A healthy, balanced diet • The digestive system • Teeth • The excretory system • Reading: Happy Birthday, Professor Eco! • Writing: What did you eat yesterday?	• How does the digestive system work?
Unit 2 **Our body**	• Growing up • The circulatory system and the heart • The respiratory system and the lungs • The reproductive system • How we're born • Reading: Yousef's surprise • Writing: Growing up	• How does the heart work? • How do we breathe?
Unit 3 **Animals**	• Mammals • Birds • Fish and amphibians • Invertebrates • Reptiles • Reading: The invertebrates hunt! • Writing: Animals in my environment	• Which animals live near you?
Unit 4 **Plants**	• Plants around us • Pollination and fertilisation • How plants make their own food • Reading: The beehives • Writing: Pollination	• How does photosynthesis work?
Units 1–4 **Review**	• Science Club Quiz • Science Challenge	
Unit 5 **Our planet**	• The solar system • The Earth's moon • The Earth's rotation and orbit • Our planet • The Earth's year • Climate on Earth • Reading: The solar eclipse • Writing: The climate where I live	• Why does the Earth have different seasons?
Unit 6 **Energy**	• Forms of energy • Light • Sound • Renewable and non-renewable energy • Reading: The world of mirrors • Writing: How I use energy	• Do hot things contain more energy than cold things? • How does light interact with an object? • Why do shadows change shape?

	Content	Let's investigate!
Unit 7 **Machines**	• We need machines • Simple machines • Complex machines • How a complex machine works • Reading: The Science Fair • Writing: An important invention	• How does a pulley work?
Unit 8 **Matter**	• Matter is all around us • Changes in matter • Mixtures • Properties of materials • Natural and manufactured materials • The three Rs • Reading: The Science Club recycling centre • Writing: Materials around me	• What chemical change can happen to an apple? • Can you separate the substances in a heterogeneous mixture? • What solids form a homogeneous mixture with water?
Units 5–8 **Review**	• Science Club Quiz • Science Challenge	
Unit 9 **Living together**	• The school community • The area where we live • Emergency services • Provinces and Autonomous Communities • The organisation of Autonomous Communities • Autonomous Communities are different • Reading: The forest fire • Writing: My letter to the Mayor	• Find out about your Autonomous Community.
Unit 10 **Our country**	• We live in a democracy • The organisation of Spain • The geography of Spain • Reading a relief map • Reading: The volcano • Writing: My Autonomous Community	• How can you elect a Class President?
Unit 11 **Population**	• Classifying population • Population changes • A growing population • Reading: A new pupil • Writing: Create a class census	• How can you classify the population of your household?
Unit 12 **History**	• Changing times • Prehistory • Ancient history • The Middle Ages • The Modern Age • The Contemporary Age • Reading: Treasure! • Reading: A building from the past	• Do you know about these important people in history?
Units 9–12 **Review**	• Science Club Quiz • Science Challenge	

What we already know

Look at the photos. How much can you remember?

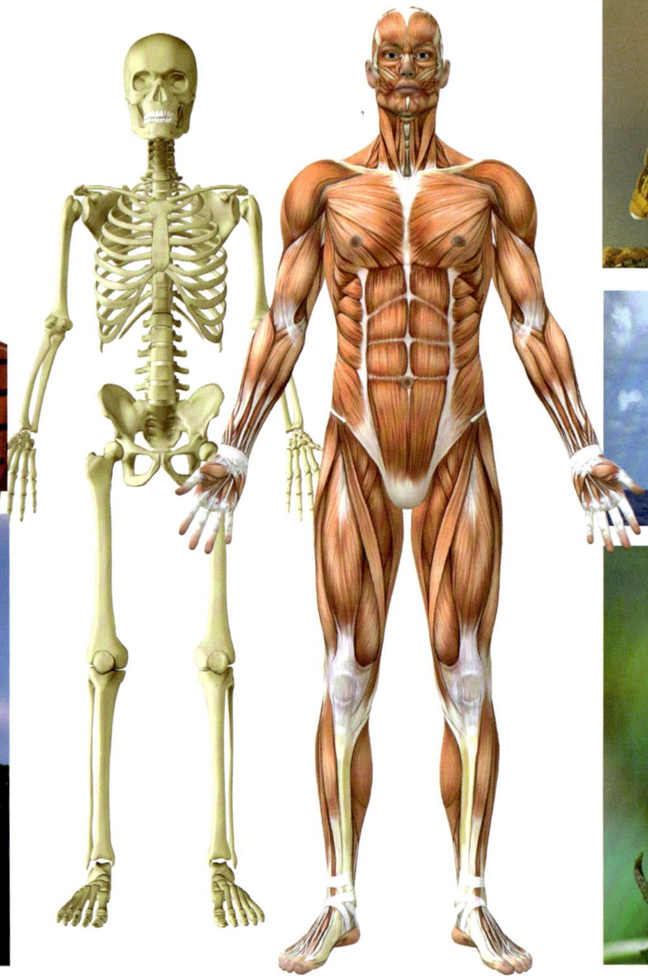

I know about the life processes of living things. ☆ ☆ ☆

I know about the sense organs. ☆ ☆ ☆

I know about muscles and bones. ☆ ☆ ☆

I know about vertebrates and invertebrates. ☆ ☆ ☆

I know about the parts of plants and their functions. ☆ ☆ ☆

I know about different habitats. ☆ ☆ ☆

I know about water and air. ☆ ☆ ☆

I know about different landscapes. ☆ ☆ ☆

I know about soil, rocks and minerals. ☆ ☆ ☆

I know about different forms of transport and communication. ☆ ☆ ☆

I know about jobs in the primary, secondary and tertiary sectors. ☆ ☆ ☆

I know about villages, towns and cities. ☆ ☆ ☆

In this unit we're going to learn about food and nutrition, and how our body processes food.

What did you have for breakfast today?

Our food comes from plants or animals, but we can also classify food into these groups: **fruit and vegetables**, **bread and cereals**, **milk and dairy**, **meat and fish** and **sugary foods**. Can you remember which of these food groups isn't so good for us?

Our body needs food for **health**, **growth** and **energy**. Breakfast, lunch and dinner are the three main meals of the day. It's important to have healthy, balanced meals, and remember to eat five fruit and vegetables a day!

c
d
g
h
k
l

1 🔵 Say the *Food* chant.

2 Copy the chart and classify the foods in photos a–l.

Health	Growth	Energy

3 🔵 Identify the foods that aren't so good for us.

Nutrients

Nutrients in our food keep us healthy, help us grow and give us energy.

Vitamins are for our health.

Minerals are good for our health, too. An important mineral is **calcium**, which we need for strong and healthy bones and teeth.

Proteins are for our growth.

Carbohydrates give us energy.

Fats give us energy, too, but we only need a little of these.

Remember that our body also needs water!

1  **Say the *Nutrients* chant.**

2  **Say the *Nutrients* rap.**

3 **Look at pictures 1–5 above. Match them to a–e below.**

   a vitamins and minerals
   b calcium
   c carbohydrates
   d fats
   e proteins

4 **Which nutrient do we only need a little of?**

We only need a little …

5 **What nutrients did you eat yesterday?**

Yesterday I ate …, which gives me …

DID YOU KNOW?

An apple gives us vitamins, but most of an apple is water.

We need to have a healthy, balanced diet. A **healthy diet** means eating foods that have nutrients. We need a **balanced diet**, too. A balanced diet has lots of different nutrients. Remember! We also need to exercise to stay healthy.

breakfast

lunch

breakfast

lunch

snack

dinner

snack

dinner

1 **What's a healthy, balanced diet?**

A healthy, balanced diet has …

2 **Listen to Nico and Clara talking about what they ate today.**

Nico ate … for breakfast, he ate … for lunch, …

3 **Who do you think has the best diet? Why?**

I think … has the best diet because …

4 **What advice can you give Nico and Clara about a healthy, balanced diet?**

You should …

5 **Make a healthy meals menu for one day.**

The digestive system

CD1 9

break down *(verb)* when something separates into different parts.

Our **digestive system** allows our body to get the nutrients it needs from the food we eat.

- The digestive process starts in the **mouth**. We chew food with our teeth and mix the food with saliva.

- Our tongue pushes the food around our mouth to a tube called the **oesophagus**.

- The food travels down the oesophagus to our **stomach**. The stomach is like a mixer. It uses gastric juices to turn the food into a thick liquid.

- The thick liquid travels to a long tube called the **small intestine**. The small intestine breaks down the food mixture even more.

- The **liver** and the **pancreas** send juices to the small intestine so that our body can now absorb the nutrients in the food.

- The remains of the food that our body can't use go to a wide tube called the **large intestine**. Here our body has its last chance to take water from the food.

- The remains finally leave our body through the **anus**.

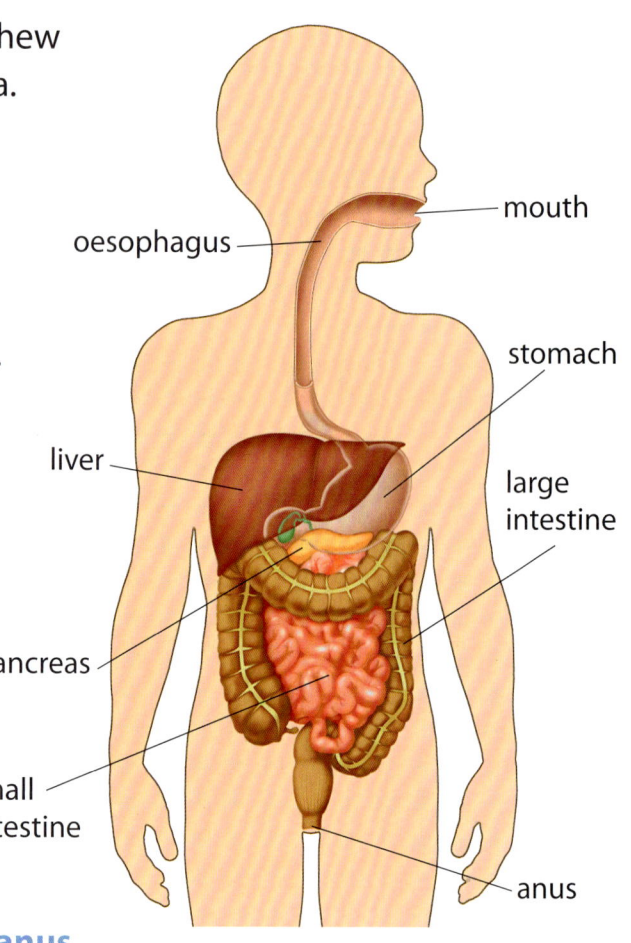

oesophagus
mouth
stomach
liver
large intestine
pancreas
small intestine
anus

1 **Say the *Digestive system* chant.**

2 **Copy and complete the digestive process diagram.**

3 **Where does the digestive process start?**
The digestive process starts in the . . .

4 **What does the stomach do?**

5 **Which organs help the small intestine break down the food mixture?**

6 **Where do the remains of the food that our body can't use go?**

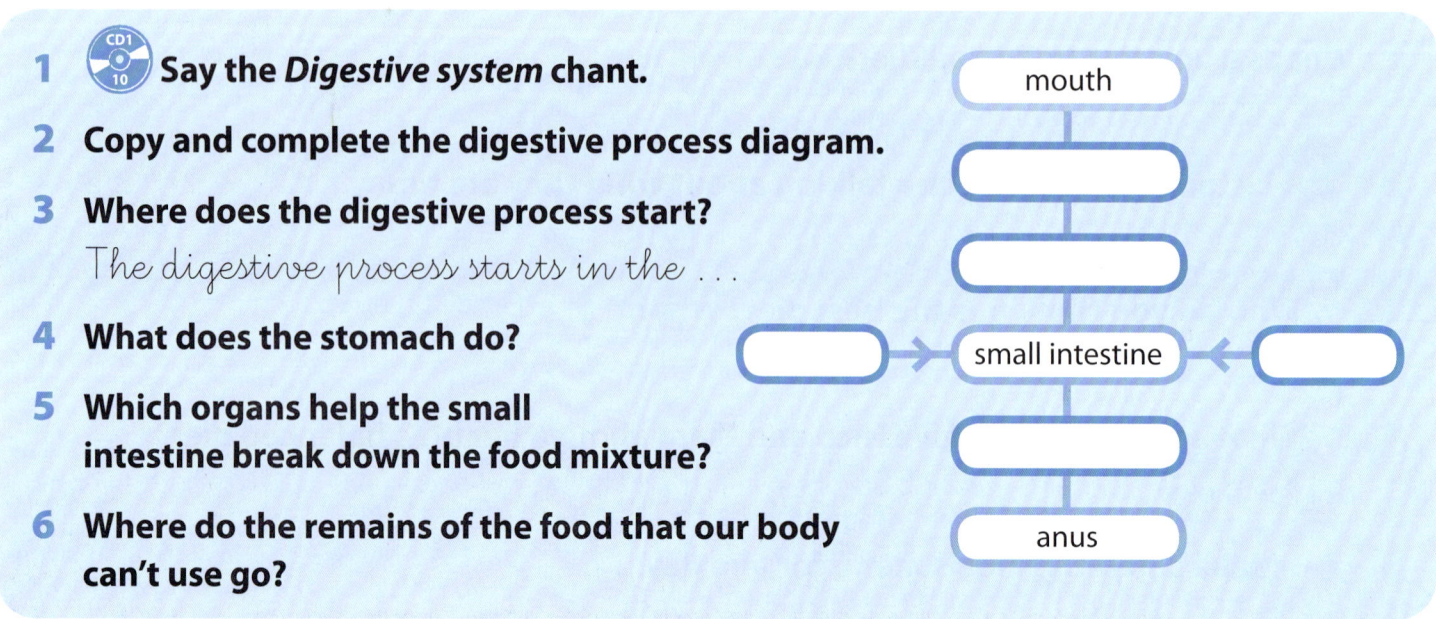

mouth

small intestine

anus

Make a model of the digestive system.

How does the digestive system work?

You need:
- card
- plasticine

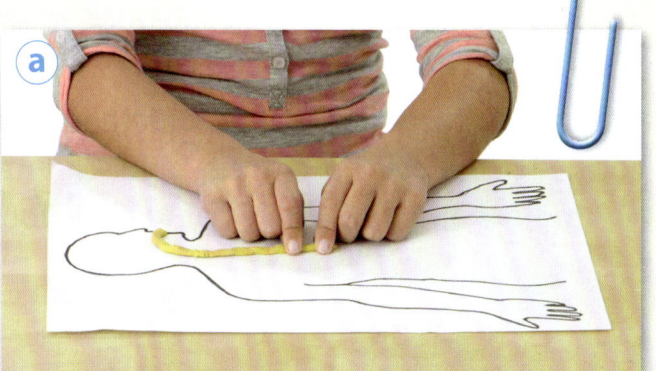

a

Make the oesophagus.

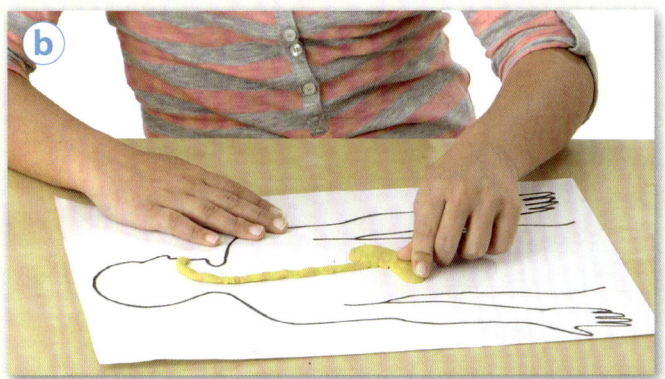

b

Next, make the stomach.

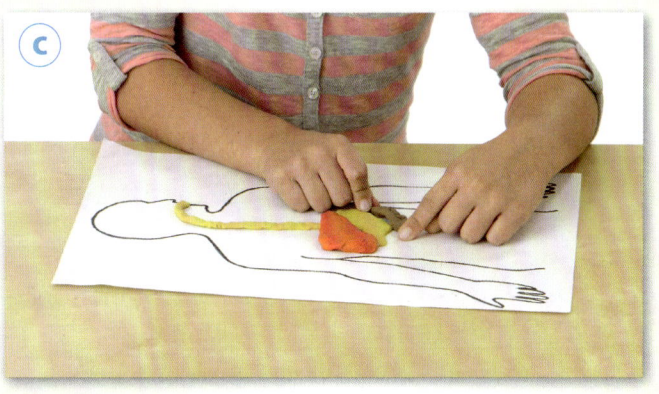

c

Now, make the liver and the pancreas.

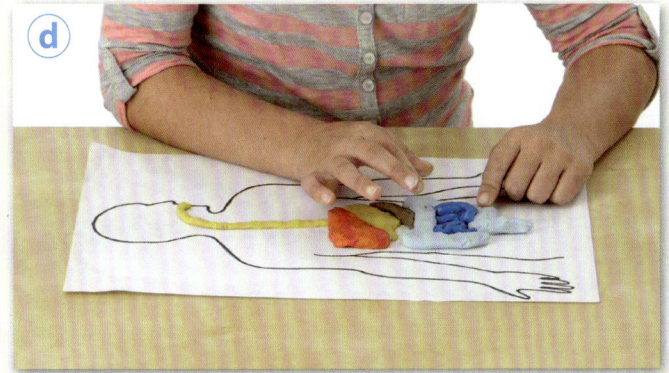

d

Finally, make the small and large intestines and the anus.

e

When you've finished, label the model.

f Present your model of the digestive system.

This is the … When we eat food, it travels from the … to the …
Then / Next / After that it travels from the … to the …

Teeth

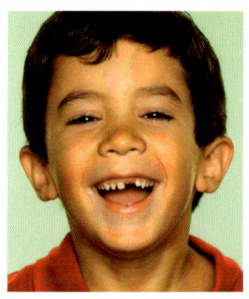

Children have twenty teeth called **milk teeth**. When we're about six years old, our milk teeth start to fall out and our **permanent teeth** start to grow. Adults have thirty-two permanent teeth and these are bigger than our milk teeth.

We use our teeth to eat food. Different types of teeth do different jobs. **Incisors** are sharp to cut food. **Canines** are pointed to tear food. **Premolars** and **molars** are flat to chew food.

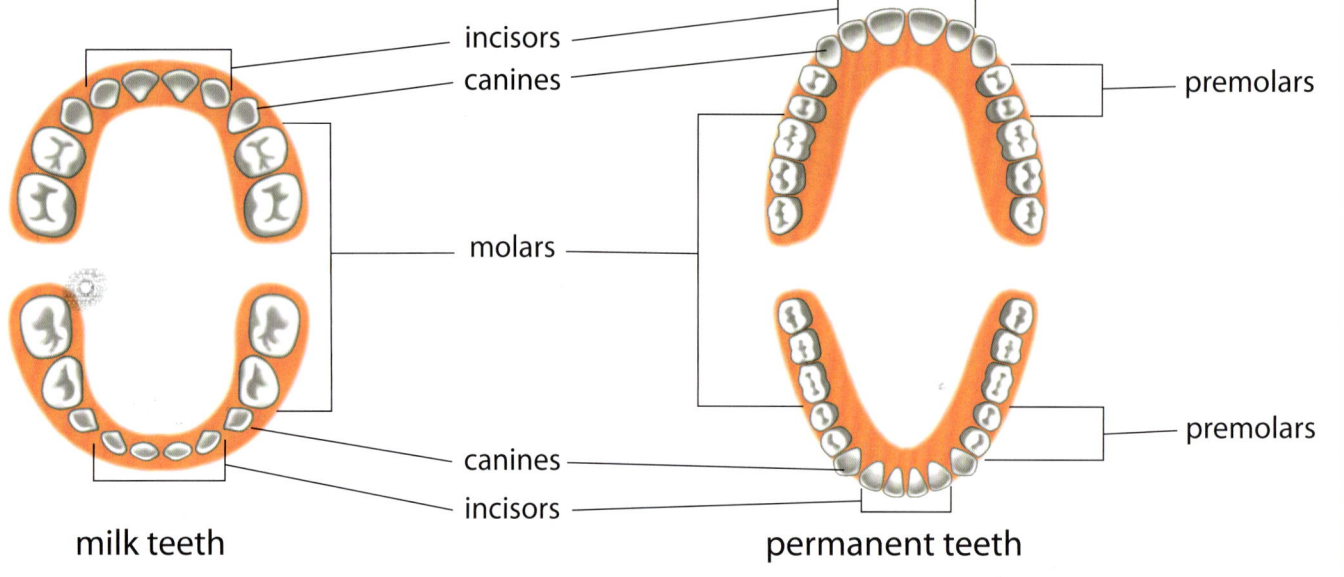

milk teeth

permanent teeth

We must look after our teeth to keep them healthy. **Brush your teeth** with toothpaste, especially after eating sweets. Sugar is bad for your teeth! It's also important to go to the **dentist** regularly.

1 Copy and complete the sentences.

a Children have _____ milk teeth.

b Our milk teeth start to fall out when we're about _____ years old.

c Adults have _____ permanent teeth.

2 Copy and correct the sentences.

a Brush your teeth before eating sweets.

b Sugar is good for your teeth!

c Never visit your dentist.

3 Identify, copy and label the teeth.

| canine | molar | incisor | premolar |

a b c d

4 ⭐Me How many permanent teeth do you have?

I have . . . permanent teeth.

We already know that the remains of the food that our body can't use leaves through the anus. Our body also needs to eliminate other waste and this is done by our **excretory system**.

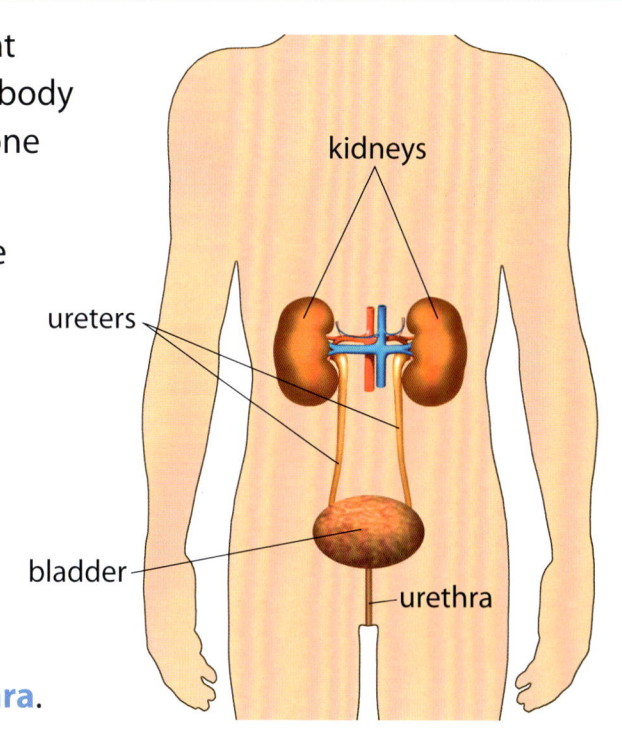

- Two small organs called the **kidneys** clean the waste from our blood.

- This waste combines with water to make **urine**.

- Urine goes down two tubes called **ureters**, and collects in a bag called the **bladder**.

- When our bladder starts to get full, our body tells us that it's time to go to the toilet.

- Urine then leaves our body through the **urethra**.

Our body also eliminates waste through the **skin**. This waste is in the form of a liquid called **sweat**. We sweat when our body temperature rises. This often happens when we do exercise. We have **sweat glands** that produce sweat all over our skin. Sweating cleans waste from our body and it also helps us keep cool if we get too hot.

1 **Copy and label the diagram of the excretory system.**

2 **Copy and match the definitions.**
  a ureters   A bag that collects urine.
  b urethra   Organs that clean the waste from our blood and make urine.
  c kidneys   Tubes that take urine to the bladder.
  d bladder   A tube that takes urine out of our body.

3 **What makes our body sweat?**

4 **Why is sweating good for our body?**

Happy Birthday, Professor Eco!

1 It's Professor Eco's birthday tomorrow. Nico is making a chocolate mousse.

I need cream.

2 I need chocolate.

USE BY 1st SEP

3 I need egg whites …

4 … and I need sugar.

USE BY 1st SEP

5 The next day …

28th September.

Happy Birthday!

Chocolate mousse! Thank you! I'll eat it at lunch.

6 After lunch …

Oh dear! My stomach hurts.

7 Where's Professor Eco?

He's ill. Nico? What did you put in the mousse?

8 Oh no! Sorry, Professor Eco.

USE BY 1st SEP

Food labels give us lots of information. They tell us when we should use the food. They also tell us where we should keep the food, as some foods need to go in the fridge or in the freezer.

Food labels identify the ingredients in the food we buy and they give us lots of information about the nutrients in our food, too.

WHAT DID YOU EAT YESTERDAY?

1 ⭐Me **Write a text about what you had for breakfast, lunch, a snack and dinner yesterday.**

  a Write a list of all the food you ate yesterday.
  b Identify the nutrients in these foods.
  c Draw a chart to classify the foods by these nutrients.
  d Draw pictures to illustrate the foods.
  e Write a text describing what you ate and decide if you had healthy, balanced meals yesterday.

MY SCIENCE PROJECT

REMEMBER!

For breakfast, I had toast.

Vitamins and minerals	Carbohydrates
orange juice	potatoes
Fats	**Proteins**
chocolate biscuits	meat

For breakfast, I had toast with jam and orange juice.

For lunch, I had lentils, meat, potatoes, spinach and water.

For a snack, I had a cheese sandwich and chocolate biscuits.

For dinner, I had fish, salad and an apple.

1 **Copy and complete the word maps.**

bread and cereals   proteins   milk and dairy
calcium   carbohydrates   sugary foods

Food groups

| fruit and vegetables | meat and fish | | | |

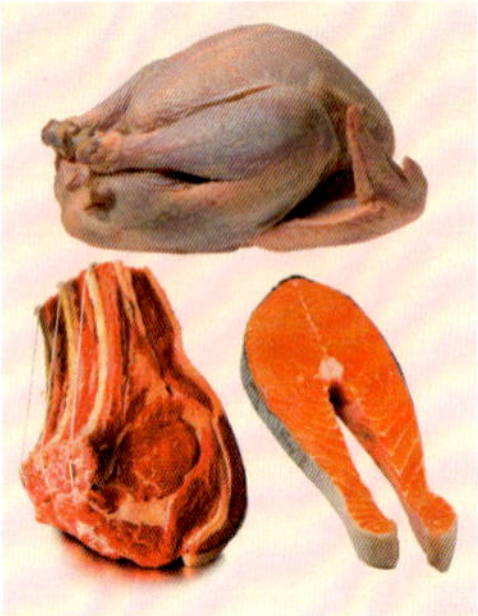

Nutrients

vitamins and minerals

| | | fats | | |

2 **Use the word maps to copy and complete the sentences.**

We can classify food into five groups: _____ , _____ , bread and cereals, _____ and sugary foods. There are nutrients in food. Vitamins and minerals are good for our health. _____ are for our growth. _____ give us energy. _____ give us energy, too, but we only need a little of these.

3 **Copy the chart and classify the food.**

chicken   milk   sweets   bread   chocolate
cheese   green beans   oranges   pasta   sardines

Bread and cereals	Fruit and vegetables	Meat and fish

Milk and dairy	Sugary foods

4 **Copy and complete the sentences about teeth.**

a   are sharp to cut food.

b   are pointed to tear food.

c   and   are flat to chew food.

5 **Copy and complete the sentences about the excretory system.**
a   The   clean the waste from our blood and make urine.
b   The   take the urine to the bladder.
c   The   collects the urine.
d   The   takes the urine out of our body.

6 **What do we call the waste liquid that our body eliminates through the skin?**

I know about nutrients and a healthy, balanced diet.   ☆ ☆ ☆

I understand how the digestive system works.   ☆ ☆ ☆

I can identify different types of teeth.   ☆ ☆ ☆

I understand how the excretory system works.   ☆ ☆ ☆

In this unit we're going to look inside our body and learn about the circulatory system, the respiratory system and the reproductive system.

What stage of life are you at now?

a

d

We all **look different** and **change** as we **get older**, but we all have the **same systems inside our body**. These systems allow us to carry out life processes.

There are different **stages of life**. When we're born, we're **babies** and we need our parents to do everything for us. Babies eat, sleep and discover the world around them. We grow into **children** and we learn many things. We can walk, talk and play. When we're **adolescents**, our body continues to grow and change. When we're **adults**, our body stops growing. Many adults reproduce and have families. Finally, we're **elderly**. Elderly people sometimes need us to look after them. Remember, elderly people have a lot of experience and we must respect them.

b

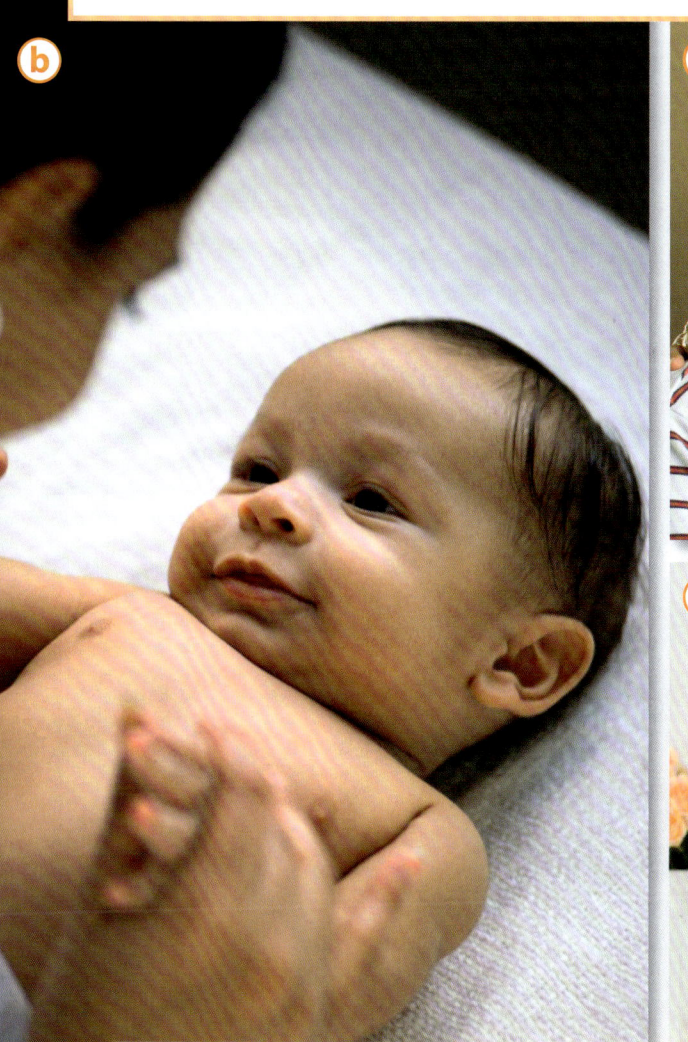

c

e

1 Look at photos a–e. Compare and contrast the people.

2 Order the people in the photos from the youngest to the oldest.

3 Identify the stages of life in the photos.

Photo … is a baby.

4 **Me** What stages of life are you and your family at now?

I'm a … My sister is … My mother is …

The circulatory system and the heart

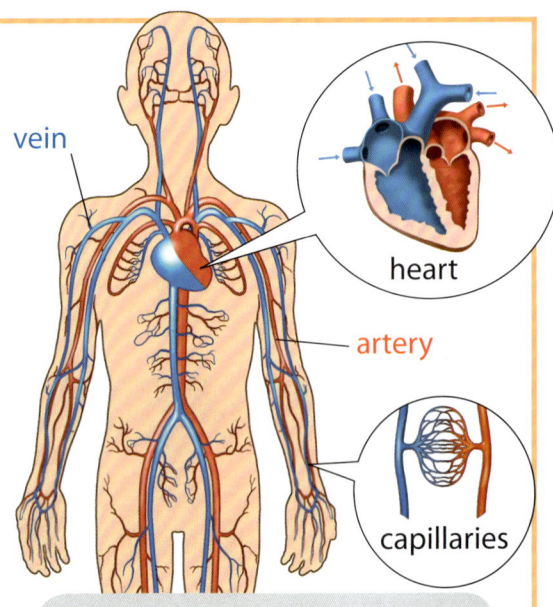

vein

heart

artery

capillaries

The **circulatory system** moves blood through the **heart** and around our body. The blood gives our body the oxygen and nutrients it needs. Blood also carries waste that we need to eliminate from our body.

The heart is an organ made up of very strong involuntary muscles. It contracts and relaxes to pump blood through the **blood vessels** in our body. There are three types of blood vessels . **Arteries** carry blood and nutrients from the heart to all parts of our body. **Veins** carry blood back to the heart from the rest of our body. **Capillaries** are very small vessels that connect our arteries and veins.

vessel *(noun)* a tube in living things that liquid flows through.

Let's investigate! — The heart

 **Investigate what happens when our heart beats.**

How does the heart work?

You need:
- a sponge
- red food colouring
- water
- a bowl

a Squeeze the sponge. This is the heart contracting.

b Let go of the sponge. This is the heart relaxing.

1 Say the *Circulatory system* chant.

2 **Copy and match the definitions.**

   a arteries   These are very small vessels that connect our arteries and veins.
   b capillaries   These carry blood back to the heart from the rest of our body.
   c veins   These carry blood and nutrients from the heart to all parts of our body.

3  **What can you do to look after your heart?**

The **respiratory system** is made up of organs that help us breathe. We **breathe in oxygen** from the air and we **breathe out carbon dioxide**.

We breathe in air through our **nose** and **mouth**.

The **pharynx** opens and the air goes down a tube called the **trachea**.

The air then travels down two tubes called **bronchi** and enters the **lungs**.

The oxygen from the air passes from the lungs into our **blood**.

Carbon dioxide from our body passes from our blood into the lungs. When we breathe out, the carbon dioxide leaves our lungs.

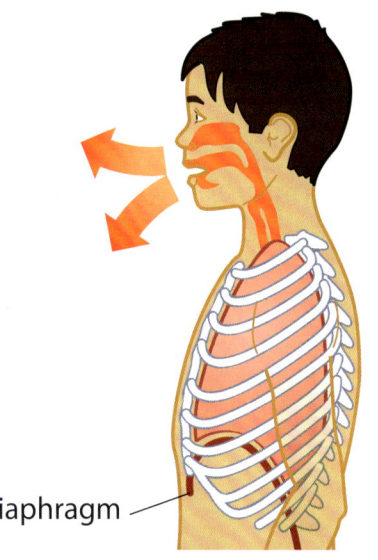

trachea

pharynx

bronchi

diaphragm

lungs

We breathe in oxygen from the air. A sheet of muscle called the **diaphragm** contracts when we breathe in to allow our lungs to fill with air.

We breathe out carbon dioxide. The diaphragm relaxes when we breathe out.

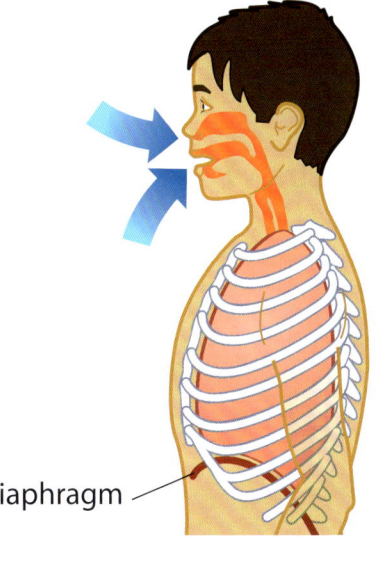

diaphragm

diaphragm

1 Say the *Respiratory system* chant.

2 How many lungs do we have?

3 Copy and write the correct sentences.

  a Our lungs get **bigger** / **smaller** when we breathe in.

  b Our lungs get **bigger** / **smaller** when we breathe out.

4 Order the parts of the respiratory system to show how oxygen passes into our blood.

lungs   pharynx   nose

bronchi   blood   trachea

5 Describe how carbon dioxide travels from our blood into the air.

6 Sing the *Circulatory and respiratory systems* song.

Make a model of the respiratory system.

You need:

- a plastic bottle with the bottom cut off
- a plastic bag
- two balloons
- two straws
- sellotape
- scissors
- plasticine

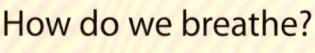

How do we breathe?

a

Tape balloons to the ends of two straws.

b

Place the straws in the bottle. Secure them with plasticine at the top of the bottle.

c

Cut the plastic bag and stick it over the bottom of the bottle.

d

Blow into the straws.

e What does the plastic bag represent?

f What do the two balloons represent?

g What do the straws represent?

h Write the correct sentences.

1 When we breathe in, the diaphragm **contracts** / **relaxes**.

2 When we breathe out, the diaphragm **contracts** / **relaxes**.

The reproductive system

As we grow up, our body starts to change and our **reproductive organs** develop. Our reproductive system makes it possible for us to have babies. We already know about some of the organs in the human body, but men and women have different reproductive systems. These two reproductive systems need to work together so that we can reproduce.

The **male reproductive organs** are on the inside and the outside of the body.

The **testicles** store and produce **sperm**. The testicles are located in a bag called the **scrotum**. The **penis** is connected to the testicles by small tubes. The **urethra** is a tube in the penis. Sperm travels through the urethra to the outside of the body.

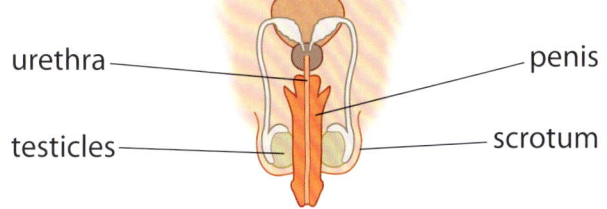

urethra — penis

testicles — scrotum

The **female reproductive organs** are mostly inside the body.

The **ovaries** store and produce **eggs**. The **uterus** is connected to the ovaries by tubes. The **vagina** is a muscular tube. It connects the uterus to the outside of the body. The **vulva** is on the outside of the body and covers the opening to the vagina.

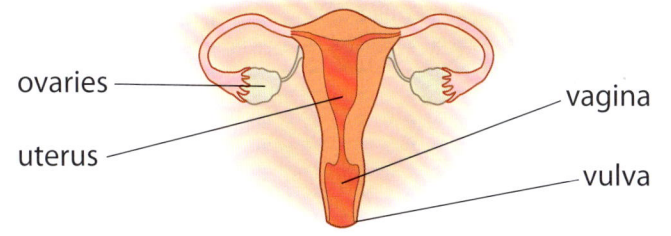

ovaries — vagina

uterus — vulva

1 Look at the photos of the man and the woman. How are their bodies different?

2 Say the *Reproductive systems* chant.

3 Copy the chart and classify the parts of the male and female reproductive systems.

uterus penis scrotum vagina ovaries testicles vulva urethra

Male reproductive organs	Female reproductive organs

4 What do the testicles and the ovaries produce?

DID YOU KNOW?

When sperm joins an egg, a baby starts to grow in the uterus.

How we are born

Reproduction begins with **fertilisation**. This is when a sperm joins an egg. The next stage is **pregnancy**. This is when the baby starts to develop in the uterus. A human pregnancy lasts nine months. The final stage is **birth**. This is when the baby leaves the uterus and is born.

Fertilisation

①

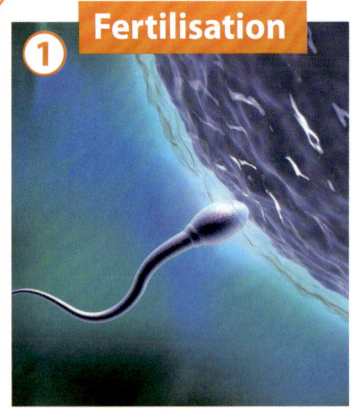

A sperm joins an egg.

In the first three months …

②

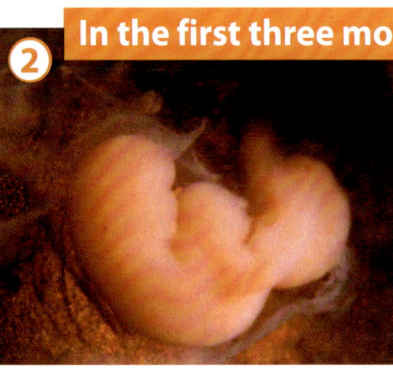

The embryo is about the size of a small seed.

③

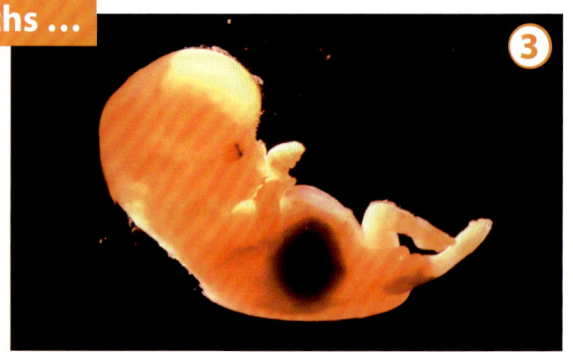

The embryo becomes a foetus. The foetus is about the size of a bean.

In the first three months …

④

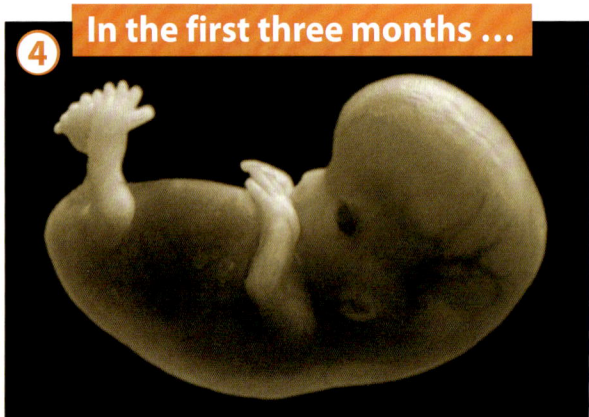

Limbs start to grow and organs start to develop.

In the second three months …

⑤

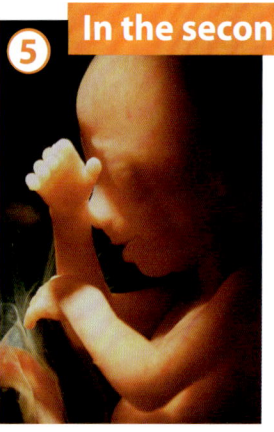

The face starts to form.

⑥

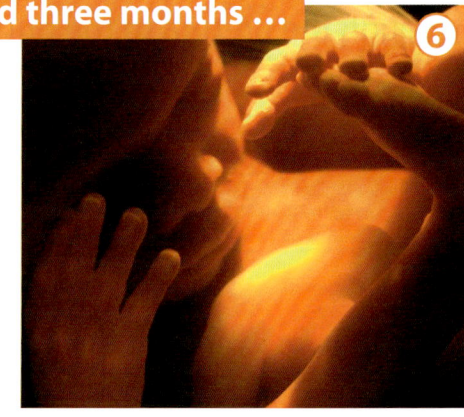

The foetus has all its organs and it continues to grow.

In the last three months …

⑦

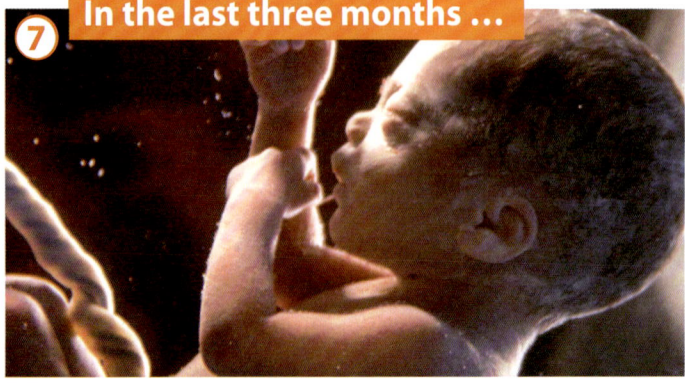

The foetus is developed and preparing to be born.

Birth

⑧

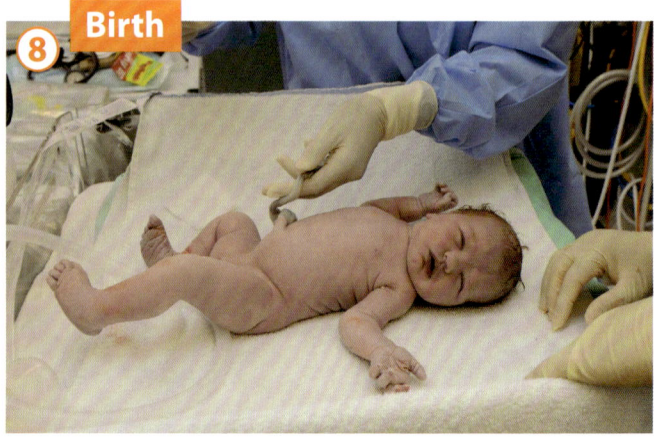

The baby is born.

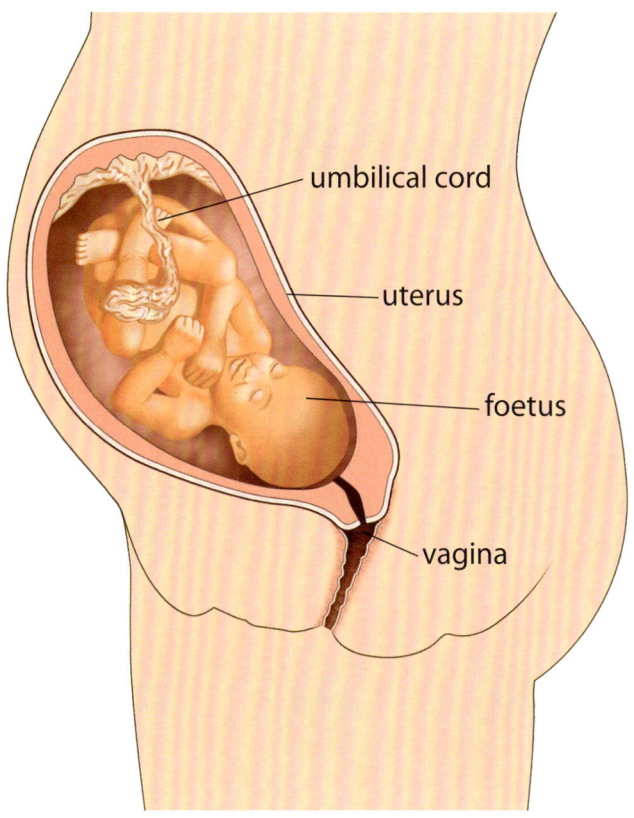

The umbilical cord transports nutrients from the mother to the foetus.

1 **Copy and write the definitions.**

   a When the baby leaves the uterus and is born.

   b When a sperm joins an egg.

   c When the baby develops in the uterus.

2 **How long does a human pregnancy last?**

   A human pregnancy lasts . . .

3 **Look at the picture of the pregnant woman and describe the foetus.**

4 **How does the baby leave its mother's body?**

Discover

How long are these animal pregnancies?

   a elephant

   b cat

   c dolphin

Yousef's surprise

1 Yousef has some news for his friends.

Guess what? I'm going to have a baby brother or sister.

Wow! That's great!

2 Six months later …

Look! This is my present for the new baby.

And this is my present for the new baby.

3 Nico! Clara! My mother's here. Bring your presents!

4 This is my present!

A teddy bear! Thank you, Nico.

5 Sorry! It's the same.

Don't worry, Clara. Look.

6 Say hello to my baby brother.

And my baby sister.

Oh twins!

Sometimes two babies are born in one pregnancy and we call them **twins**. Twins sometimes look exactly the same, but other times they're different. When twins look exactly the same we call them **identical** twins, but when they look different we call them **non-identical** twins. Non-identical twins can be two boys, two girls, or a boy and a girl. Identical twins develop when a fertilised egg becomes two embryos. Non-identical twins develop when two eggs are fertilised at the same time.

GROWING UP

1  **Find photos of you growing up. Order the photos from the youngest to the oldest. Write a text for each photo.**

   a What did you look like?   **b** What could you do?

2  **Describe yourself now.**

   a What do you look like?   **b** What can you do?

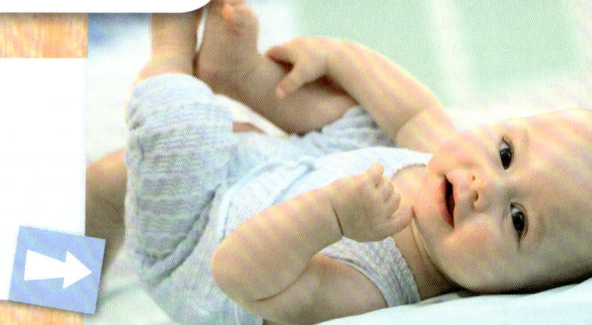

This is me when I was a baby.
I was very small.
I slept, I cried and I drank milk.

This is me when I was one year old.
I had blond hair.
I could crawl and smile.

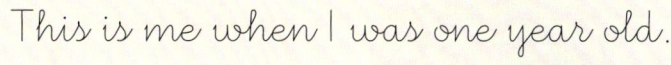

This is me when I was two years old.
I could walk, play with toys and talk, too!

This is me when I was five years old.
I could kick a ball, I could catch a ball and I could count!

REMEMBER!

When I **was** two years old ...

This is me now. I'm 1 m 40 cm tall and I weigh 32 kg.
I have short, brown hair and brown eyes.
I can run fast and I can ride a bike.
I can read, write and speak English.

1 **Copy and complete the word maps.**   lungs   veins   trachea   arteries

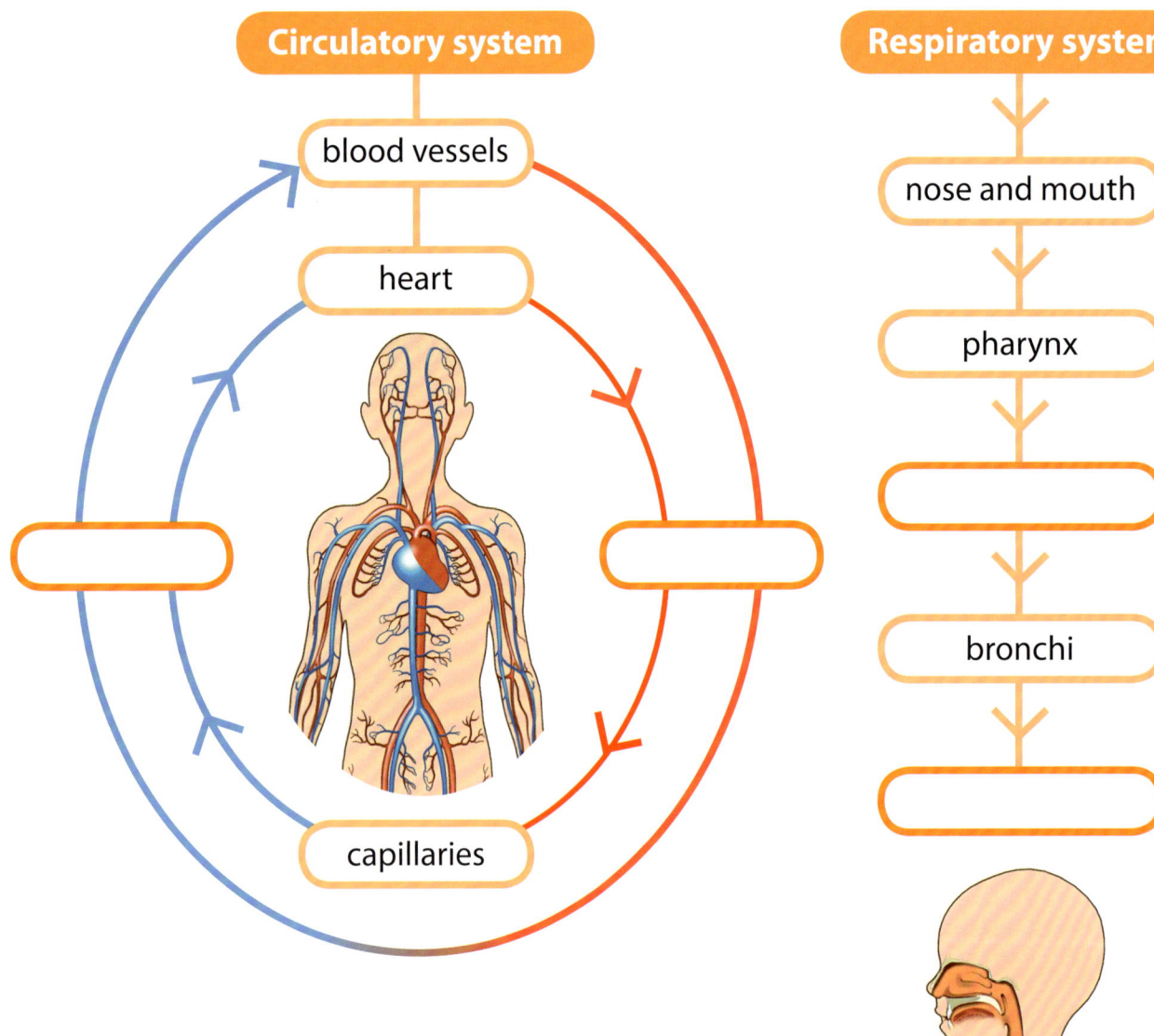

Circulatory system

blood vessels

heart

capillaries

Respiratory system

nose and mouth

pharynx

bronchi

2 **Use the word maps to copy and complete the sentences.**

a The circulatory system includes the heart and three types of blood ▭ : veins, arteries and ▭ .

b The respiratory system is made up of the pharynx, a tube called the trachea, two tubes called ▭ and two lungs.

3 **Order and copy the stages of life from the youngest to the oldest.**

adolescents   babies   elderly people   children   adults

4 **Copy and match the definitions.**

a arteries   These carry blood to the heart.

b veins   These connect arteries and veins.

c capillaries   These carry blood from the heart.

5 **Copy and complete the sentences about the respiratory system.**

a We breathe in ▨▨▨▨ from the air.

b The diaphragm ▨▨▨▨ when we breathe in.

c We breathe out ▨▨▨▨ ▨▨▨▨ .

d The diaphragm ▨▨▨▨ when we breathe out.

6 **Which is the odd one out? Why?**

a **penis / scrotum / vulva**

b **testicles / ovaries / vagina**

c **vulva / uterus / sperm**

d **eggs / penis / scrotum**

. . . is the odd one out because . . .

7 **Copy and complete the sentences.**

Birth   Fertilisation   Pregnancy

a ▨▨▨▨ is when a sperm joins an egg.

b ▨▨▨▨ is when a baby develops in the uterus.

c ▨▨▨▨ is when the baby leaves the uterus and is born.

I can identify and describe the stages of life.   ☆ ☆ ☆

I understand how the circulatory system works.   ☆ ☆ ☆

I understand how the respiratory system works.   ★ ☆ ☆

I know the differences between the male and female reproductive systems.   ☆ ☆ ☆

In this unit we're going to learn more about different animal groups.

This mammal has wings and it can fly! What is it?

There are all sorts of **mammals**. They can be very big like whales or elephants, or very small like mice.

Mammals have a backbone, which means that they're **vertebrates**, and most mammals have a protective covering of **fur** or hair. They breathe in oxygen from the air with their **lungs**.

Mammals are **viviparous**, which means that they give birth to live babies. All baby mammals **drink their mother's milk** until they can find their own food. Most mammals have **four legs** and move on land, but some mammals have **flippers** to move in water.

Mammals can be **carnivores**, **herbivores** or **omnivores**, and they have different types of teeth depending on the food they eat.

Tigers have striped fur and they also have striped skin!

e

f

g

h

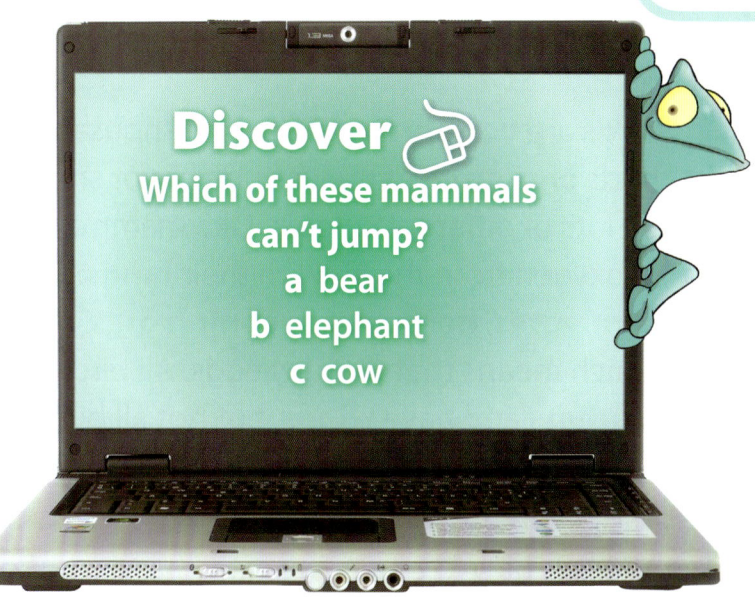

Discover
Which of these mammals can't jump?
a bear
b elephant
c cow

1 Say the *Mammals* chant.

2 **Look at photos a–h and describe these mammals.**
This animal is an elephant. It has four legs and lives on land. It has hair.

3 **What are the characteristics of mammals?**
Mammals have …
Mammals are …

4 **Which of these characteristics are unique to mammals?**

5 **Look at photos a–h. How do these mammals move? Which parts of their body do they use?**
Elephants walk. They use their legs.

6 **Can you think of a mammal that uses two legs to move?**

7 **What types of teeth do you think carnivores, herbivores and omnivores have? Why?**

Birds are vertebrates. There are thousands of types of birds on Earth and they can be big or small, and they can be lots of different colours. Like mammals, birds breathe in oxygen from the air with their lungs. Birds can be carnivores, herbivores or omnivores. They're oviparous, which means that they lay eggs. All birds are covered in feathers and have wings, but not all birds can fly!

All birds have a beak. The eagle has a hooked beak for tearing meat. Birds that eat nuts and seeds have short beaks. Birds that catch fish have long, sharp beaks, and birds that eat nectar from flowers have long, thin beaks.

DID YOU KNOW?

Ostriches can't fly, but they can run faster than people!

1 **True or false? Copy the sentences and correct the ones that are false.**
   a   Birds are vertebrates.
   b   All birds are carnivores.
   c   Not all birds have feathers and wings.
   d   All birds can fly.

2 **Can you name three birds that can't fly?**

3 **How are birds different from mammals?**
   Birds are different from mammals because . . .

4 **Look at photos a–d of the birds' beaks. Which birds eat these foods? How do you know this?**

   fish   meat

   nuts and seeds

   nectar from flowers

Fish are **vertebrates**. They have **fins** and **scales** and they breathe through their **gills**. Fish live in freshwater or in sea water and there are a few fish that can live in both freshwater and sea water. Most fish are **oviparous**, but some are **viviparous**. Fish can be **carnivores**, **herbivores** or **omnivores**.

Amphibians are **cold-blooded vertebrates**. They're **oviparous** and they lay their eggs in water. Baby amphibians live and grow in water and breathe through their **gills**. In a process called **metamorphosis**, baby amphibians change and grow into adult amphibians. Adult amphibians live in water and on land. They breathe with their **lungs** and **absorb oxygen** through their **moist skin**. Most amphibians are **carnivores**. They eat invertebrates like insects and worms, and they sometimes eat small vertebrates, too.

1 **Look at the photo of the fish and identify parts a–c.**

2 **What are the characteristics of fish?**

Fish are … Fish have … Fish live in …

3 **What are the characteristics of amphibians?**

Amphibians are … Amphibians live in … Amphibians eat …

4 **Compare the characteristics of fish and amphibians. How are they the same and how are they different?**

Fish and amphibians are the same because … Fish and amphibians are different because …

5 **Look at pictures a–e of the life cycle of a frog and describe the stages of metamorphosis.**

The first stage of metamorphosis is …

Invertebrates

Invertebrates are all around us! They live on land and in water. They walk, swim, crawl and fly. They can be big or small, but they all have one thing in common: they **don't have a backbone**. Many invertebrates have an **exoskeleton** or a **shell** to protect their body, but some invertebrates just have a **soft body**.

Insects have an exoskeleton and their body is divided into three parts: the head, the thorax and the abdomen. They have two antennae, six legs and most insects have wings.

Spiders have a body that is divided into two parts: the head and the abdomen. All spiders have eight legs and most spiders have eight eyes, but some can have six, four or two eyes.

Crabs have ten legs and two eyes. They usually move sideways, but they can move in all directions. Crabs have a thick exoskeleton.

Centipedes have lots of legs and many body parts. They have two antennae and they can move very quickly.

Worms have a soft body that is divided into many parts. An earthworm has no lungs and breathes in oxygen through its moist skin.

Octopuses have a soft body and eight legs. They have a very good sense of touch in their suckers .

Snails have a head with two tentacles and there is an eye at the end of each tentacle. Snails have a soft body that's protected by a shell.

sucker *(noun)* a round body part on some animals that they use to stick to things.

1 **What's the common characteristic of all invertebrates?**

2 **Look at the photos. Do these invertebrates live on land or in water? How do they move?**

3 **Which of these invertebrates has a shell or an exoskeleton?**

4 (CD1 40) **Sing the *Invertebrates* song.**

5 **Look at photos a–c. Identify and describe these invertebrates.**

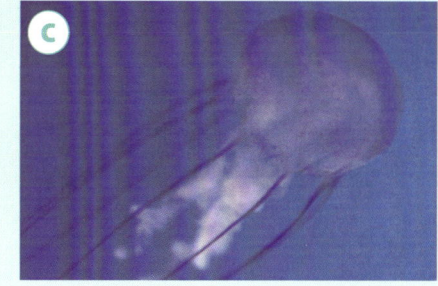

Millions of years ago, **reptiles** were the first **vertebrates** to leave the water and live on land. Most reptiles have **four limbs**. Reptiles have **scales** that cover and protect their body. Reptiles breathe in oxygen with their **lungs**. They're **cold-blooded**, which means that they can't control their body temperature and need the right environment for warmth. They get warmth from the Sun during the day and find shelter at night from the cold.

Most reptiles are **oviparous** and lay their eggs on land. Most reptiles are also **carnivores**, and they swallow their food without chewing it.

The skin of **snakes** is different from the skin of mammals. As we grow and get bigger, our skin grows, too. But a snake's skin can't grow like our skin does, so snakes need to lose a layer of skin as they grow.

Lizards also need to replace their skin with new skin. Some lizards can also lose their tail to protect themselves from predators, but the tail usually grows back.

The scales of **crocodiles** grow as the crocodile grows. Crocodiles can move quickly both on land and in water.

Tortoises and **turtles** both have a shell. Tortoises live on land and are mostly **herbivores**. Turtles live in water, but they lay their eggs on land. Most turtles are **omnivores** and eat plants, insects and fish.

1 **Can you think of a reptile that doesn't have four limbs?**

2 **Are there reptiles in the Arctic? Why? / Why not?**

3 **How do reptiles keep warm?**

Reptiles get warmth from . . .

🔍 **Investigate animals in your environment.**

You need:
- a notebook
- a pencil or a pen

Which animals live near you?

a Identify and classify these animals.
b Describe the animals and their characteristics.
c How do these animals move?

Animal	Animal group	Description	Characteristics	How it moves
frog	amphibian	moist skin four legs	can live on land and in water oviparous breathes with its lungs carnivore	hops, crawls and swims

d Discuss the results.

1 Why do you think these animals live in your environment?
2 What's the most common animal group in your environment?

The invertebrates hunt!

1 Today, the Science Club is observing invertebrates.

Remember! Don't pick up the invertebrates or disturb their homes.

2 Is this a millipede?

No, it's a centipede. Centipedes can move quickly, but millipedes move slowly.

3 Nico, is this a butterfly or a moth?

It's a butterfly. Most butterflies fly during the day and most moths fly at night.

4 Quick! Look at this insect.

That's not an insect, it's a spider. Spiders have eight legs not six.

5 Clara! Come and look at the spider's web.

I don't like spiders, I don't like insects, and I don't like centipedes.

6 Come and look at this snail.

No, I want to read my Science book.

7 Clara! You sat on an ants' nest.

You don't like invertebrates, but they like you!

Ants are insects that live in organised communities called **colonies**. There are three types of ants in a colony: **the queen**, **the female workers** and **the males**. The queen is the only ant that can lay eggs. Ant colonies can also have **soldier ants**. These soldier ants hunt for food, defend the colony and attack other colonies.

Ants are very strong and can lift objects that weigh much more than they do. This is like you lifting a car!

ANIMALS IN MY ENVIRONMENT

1 **Choose an animal from the investigation *Animals in my environment*. Use your notes to write a text about this animal.**

    a Identify the animal group.
    b Does it have a protective covering?
    c Where does it live?
    d How does it reproduce?
    e How does it breathe?
    f Describe its body.
    g What are its characteristics?
    h How does it move?
    i What does it eat?
    j Why do you think it can live in this environment?

2 **Find photos or draw pictures to illustrate your text.**

REMEMBER!

It eats . . .
It lives . . .
It **has** . . .

The frog is an amphibian. It has moist skin and it can live on land and in water. It's oviparous and lays eggs in the water. Tadpoles come from the eggs. Tadpoles breathe through their gills and have a tail. They grow four legs and turn into frogs. This process is called metamorphosis. Adult frogs breathe with their lungs. They crawl and hop on land and they swim in water. Frogs are carnivores and they eat insects.

I think frogs live in this environment because there's a lot of freshwater.

1 **Copy and complete the word map.**

vertebrates   fish   reptiles   amphibians   mammals   birds   insects

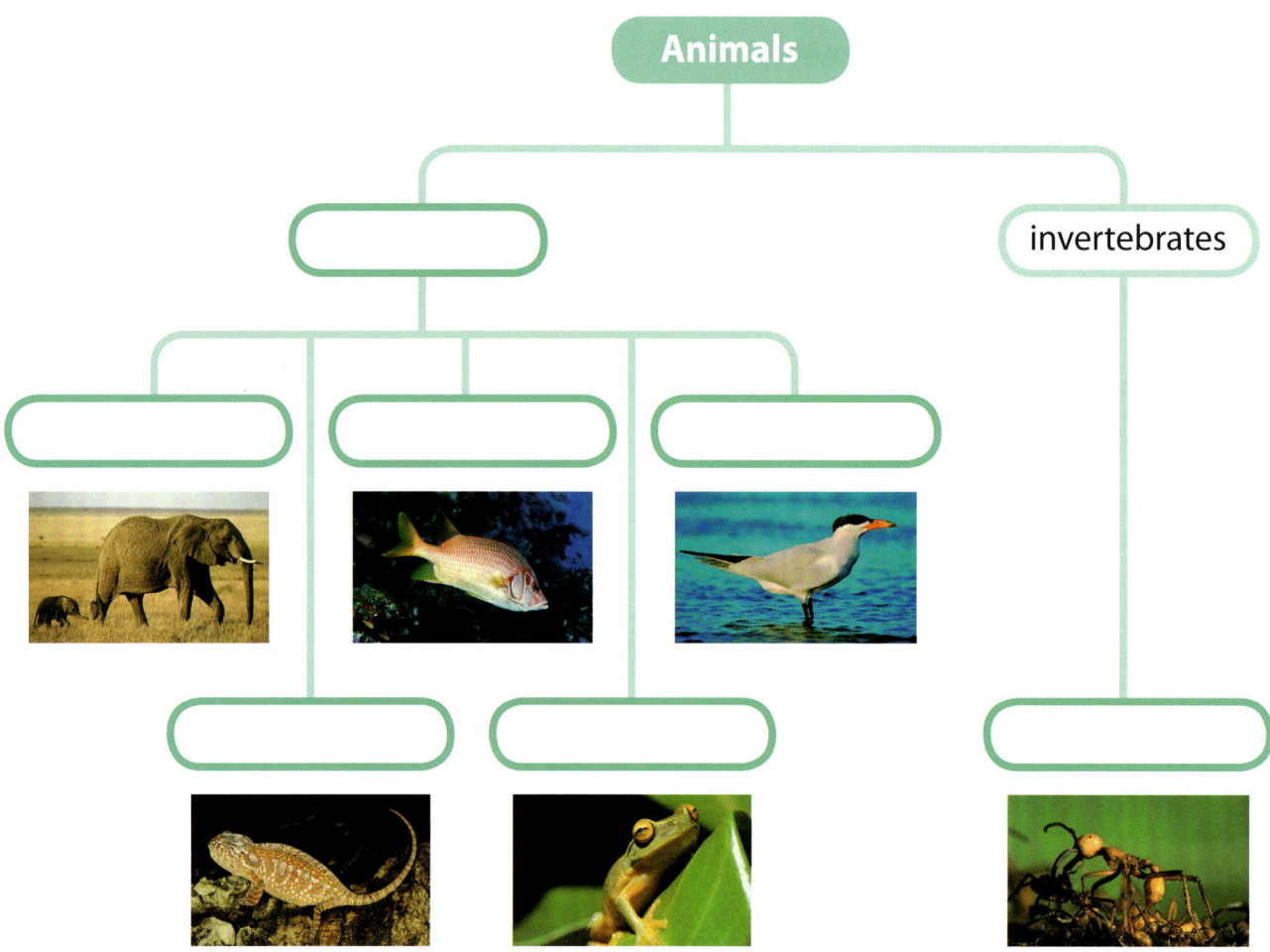

2 **Use the word map to copy and complete the sentences.**

a _____ are vertebrates. They breathe in oxygen from the air with their lungs. They're viviparous and they drink their mother's milk.

b _____ are cold-blooded vertebrates. They're oviparous and lay their eggs in water. Before they become adults, they breathe through their gills.

c _____ are vertebrates. They're oviparous and have wings.

d _____ are invertebrates. Their body is divided into three parts and they have six legs.

e _____ are cold-blooded vertebrates. They breathe in oxygen from the air with their lungs. They're oviparous and lay their eggs on land.

f _____ are cold-blooded vertebrates. They have fins and scales, and they breathe through their gills.

3 **Identify the animal groups. Which animal is the odd one out? Why?**

a whale / tiger / bear / lizard

b tortoise / snake / crocodile / snail

c shark / sardine / dolphin / seahorse

d eagle / bat / parrot / owl

e toad / salamander / chameleon / frog

f ladybird / spider / butterfly / mosquito

4 **True or false? Copy the sentences and correct the ones that are false.**

a Some mammals have flippers.

b Birds are viviparous.

c Fish breathe with their lungs.

d Adult amphibians breathe through their gills.

e Insects have four antennae.

f Reptiles are cold-blooded vertebrates.

g Invertebrates have a backbone.

5 **Copy the definitions and order the letters.**

a Amphibians absorb this through their moist skin.

nyogxe

b This is like a skeleton on the outside of the body.

keltsxooeen

c In this process, baby amphibians change and grow into adult amphibians.

moipssaoetmrh

d Some mammals have these to help them move in water.

prpslfie

e This type of animal eats plants and other animals.

vrmnoioe

 I can identify and classify animals. ☆ ☆ ☆

I know about different animal characteristics. ☆ ☆ ☆

I can describe vertebrates and invertebrates. ☆ ☆ ☆

4 Plants — Plants around us

> In this unit we're going to learn more about plants, how they reproduce and how they make their own food.

> Can you remember what plants need to grow well?

a

b

e

f

Plants are all around us and can be different shapes, sizes and colours. They give us food, medicine and clothes, and they give us the oxygen we need to live. Like all living things, plants have different life processes: **nutrition**, **interaction** and **reproduction**.

We can classify plants into **herbaceous plants**, **bushes** and **trees**. What other ways can you classify plants?

herbaceous plant *(noun)* a soft, green, low-growing plant.

1   **Why do we need plants?**
    We need plants because they give us ...

2   **Look at photos a–h. Classify the plants.**

3   **What parts of the plants can you identify?**

4   **Can you identify the different leaf margins in pictures a–f?**

Pollination and fertilisation

We already know that some plants have flowers and that the flower is the reproductive organ of a plant, but did you know that most flowers have male and female reproductive organs?

The **stamens** are the male reproductive organs and these produce **pollen**.

The **carpel** is the female reproductive organ and this includes the **stigma** and the **ovary**. The ovary produces **ovules**.

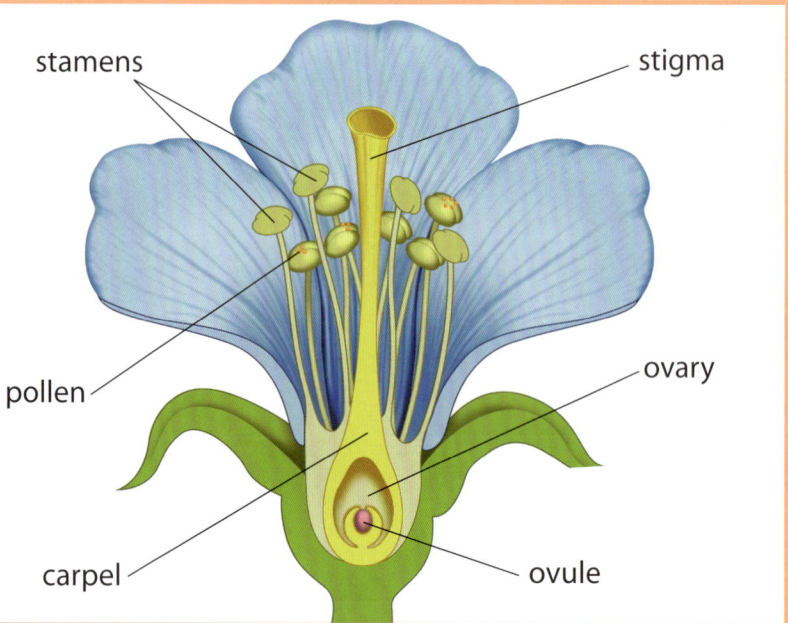

stamens

stigma

pollen

ovary

carpel

ovule

a

Pollen travels from the stamens to the stigma by animal pollination.

b

Some plants use wind pollination to reproduce.

c

The fertilised ovule becomes a seed. A fruit forms around the seed.

d

The seed germinates.

For plants to reproduce, the pollen first has to travel from the stamens to the stigma. We call this process   pollination .

Animal pollination is carried out by birds and insects, such as bees. Colourful petals attract animals to a flower. These animals come to the plant to drink a sweet liquid called **nectar**. Pollen from the stamens stick to the animal's body. When the animal travels to another plant, some of the pollen from its body is transferred to the other plant.

Wind pollination is used by plants such as trees and grasses which don't have colourful petals to attract animals. The wind blows pollen from the stamens of these plants to the stigma.

  Fertilisation   occurs when pollen joins with an ovule. This process happens in the stigma. The fertilised ovule becomes a **seed**. The stigma develops and forms a **fruit** around the seed. When a seed lands in soil it can **germinate** and a new plant grows.

DID YOU KNOW?

Most plants grow flowers every year, but *Puya raimondii* in South America only grows flowers after many years and can live for more than one hundred years!

pollination *(noun)* the transfer of pollen from the stamens to the stigma of a plant.

fertilisation *(noun)* when pollen joins with an ovule.

1  **Say the *Flower* chant.**

2 **Which parts of a flower are the male and female reproductive organs?**

The male reproductive organs of a flower are ...

3 **What do the stamens produce?**

4 **What does the ovary produce?**

5 **Copy and label the diagram of the flower.**

6 **What animals do you think can pollinate a plant?**

7 **Why do some plants use wind pollination?**

8 **Copy and complete the sentence.**
Fertilisation occurs when   joins with an   .

9 **Mark where fertilisation happens on your diagram of the flower.**

How plants make their own food

The food we eat comes from plants, but how do plants get their food?

Plants make their own food, and to do this they need **water**, **minerals**, **light and energy from the Sun** and **carbon dioxide**. The roots absorb water and minerals from the soil. The water and minerals travel up the stem to the leaves.

Plants make food in their leaves. This process is called **photosynthesis**. The leaves absorb carbon dioxide from the air through small holes. Using energy from the Sun, the carbon dioxide combines with water, minerals and sunlight to make food. During the process of photosynthesis, plants release oxygen into the air. People and animals need oxygen to breathe.

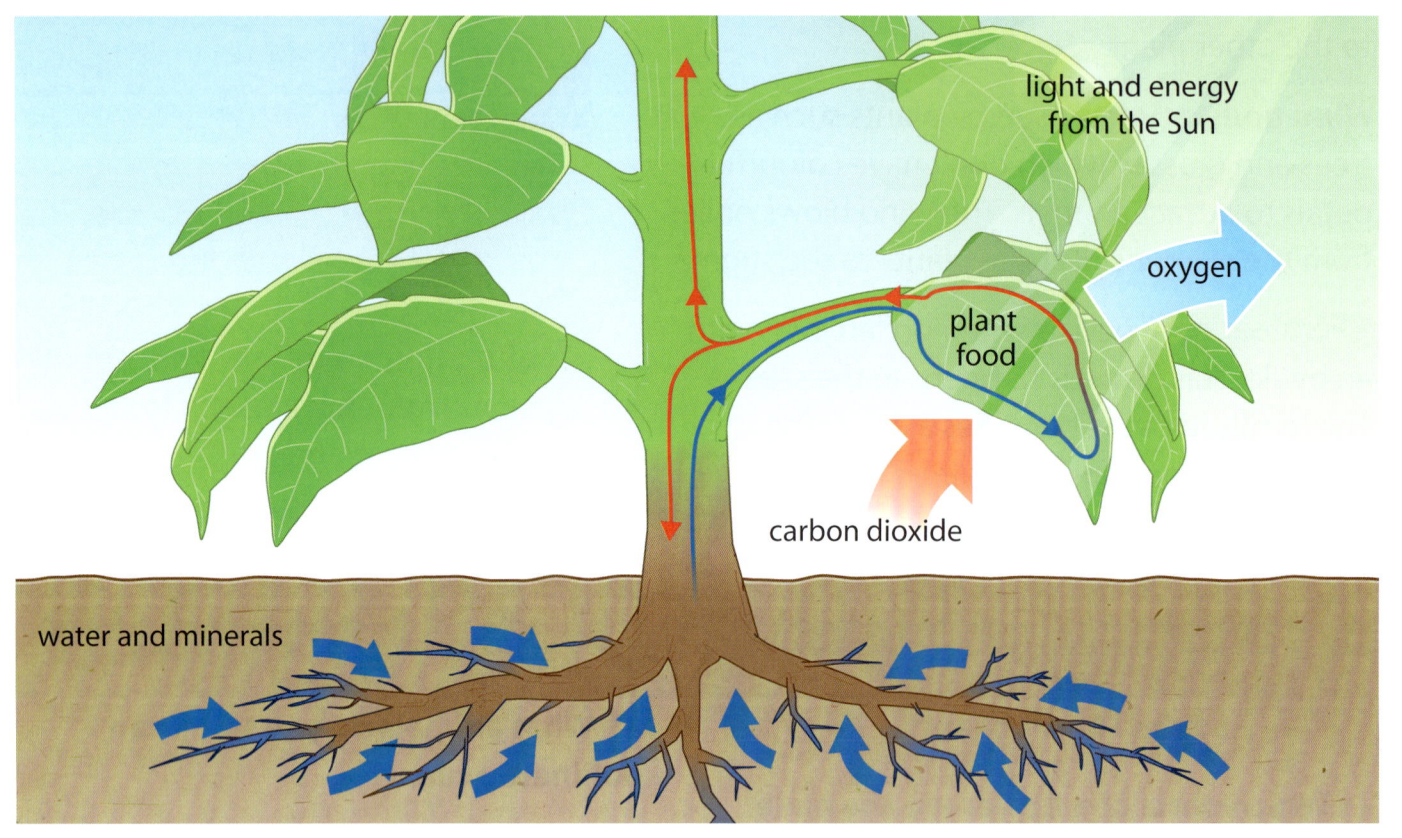

1 **What do plants need to make their own food?**

Plants need …

2 **Sing the *Photosynthesis* song.**

3 **Does photosynthesis happen during the day or at night? Why?**

Photosynthesis happens … because …

Investigate if plants need sunlight for photosynthesis.

How does photosynthesis work?

You need:

- a water plant
- a jar
- water
- a cloth

Put the plant inside the jar. Fill the jar with water.

Cover the jar with a cloth and leave for one hour.

Remove the cloth. Can you see any bubbles?

Put the jar in sunlight. Can you see any bubbles?

e Discuss the results.

1 What are the bubbles?

2 Do plants need sunlight for photosynthesis?

The beehives

1 Today, we're going to observe an insect that produces food for people.

An insect that gives us food?

2 What's that noise?

ZZZZZZ ZZZZZ

3 And what's that?

It's an alien! Help!

4 Hello! I'm a beekeeper.

We're going to observe how bees make honey.

5 Now we look like aliens, too!

6 This is a beehive, where the bees live and make honey.

So many bees!

7 Can you see the honey?

Yes, I can.

Can I taste the honey?

Of course you can, Nico.

8 I'm not Nico, I'm Yousef, but it's delicious!

People have been keeping **beehives** for thousands of years. **Honeybees** are social insects and live in colonies. Although thousands of bees live in a hive, there are only three different types of bees. The **worker bees** are female, but they can't lay eggs. These bees collect nectar from flowers and build and protect the hive. Each hive usually has one **queen bee**. The queen bee lays eggs. The **drone bees** are all male and their job is to make more bees with the queen. A queen bee can live for five years!

POLLINATION

1. **Observe and describe plants near you.**
   a. Which plants use animal pollination to reproduce?
   b. What animals pollinate the plants?
   c. Which plants use wind pollination to reproduce?

2. **Write a text using your information.**

3. **Draw pictures or use photos from magazines or the internet to illustrate your text.**

4. **Use your text and photos or pictures to make a poster.**

5. **Present your poster to the class.**

My Science Presentation

These are brightly-coloured flowers. They use animal pollination to reproduce. Bees and other insects pollinate the flower.

These are pine trees. They use wind pollination to reproduce because they don't have colourful petals to attract insects.

1 Copy and complete the word map.

stigma   ovary   stamens   pollen

Plant reproductive system

male reproductive organs

female reproductive organs

carpel

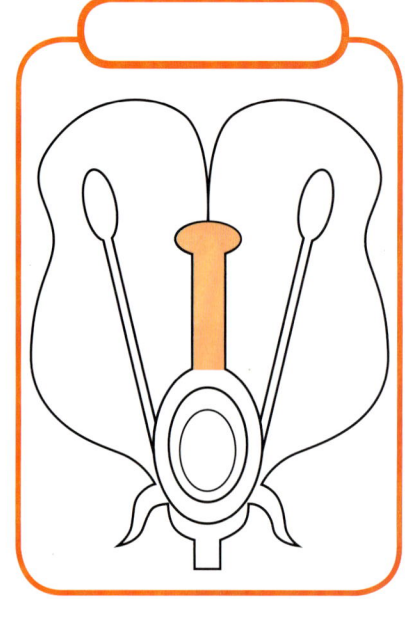

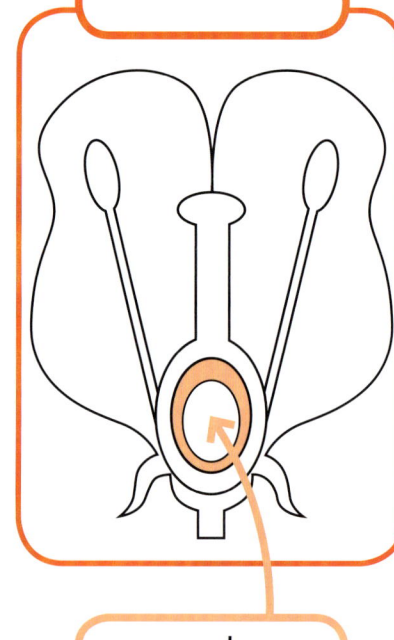

ovule

2 Use the word map to copy and complete the sentences.

a The male reproductive organs of a flower are the   .

b The stamens produce   .

c The female reproductive organ of a flower is the   .

d The carpel includes the   and the ovary.

e The ovary produces   .

3 **Copy and label the flower.**

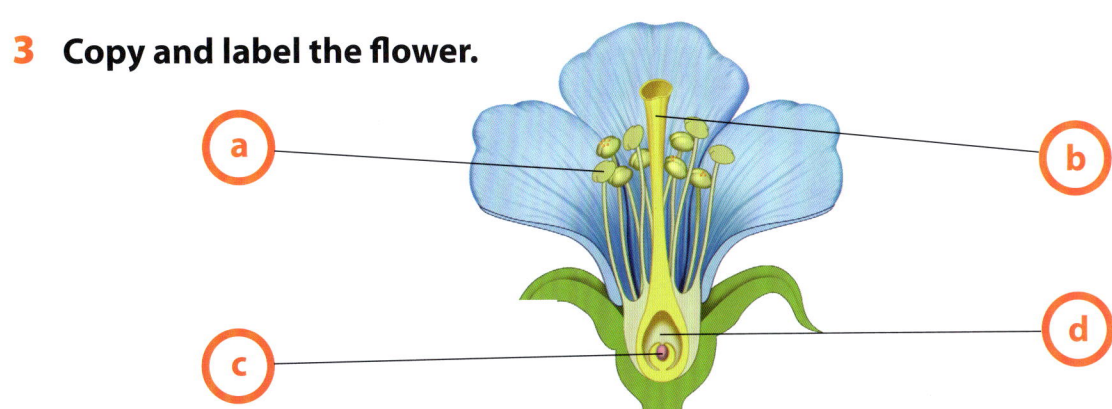

4 **Copy the definitions and write the words.**

a _____ *(noun)* the transfer of pollen from the stamens to the stigma of a plant.

b _____ *(noun)* when pollen joins with an ovule.

5 **What are two types of pollination?**

Two types of pollination are . . .

6 **Look at the picture on page 46. What do plants need to make their own food?**

7 **Copy and complete the sentence.**

During the process of photosynthesis, plants release _____ into the air.

I can identify and classify different plants.   ☆ ☆ ☆

I know how plants reproduce.   ☆ ☆ ☆

I understand how plants make their own food.   ☆ ☆ ☆

Listen to the quiz and write the answers to the questions.

SCIENCE CLUB QUIZ

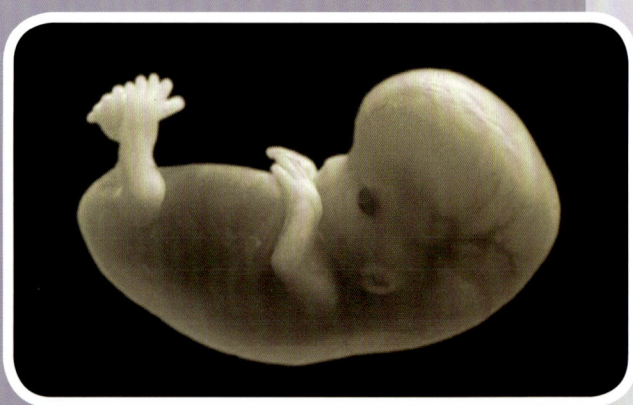

1 Name five different nutrients in our food.

2 How many teeth do children and adults have?

3 Which is longer: the small intestine or the large intestine?

4 Which system moves blood through the heart and around our body?

5 How many months does a human pregnancy normally last for?

6 What do we call animals with a backbone?

7 What do invertebrates have in common?

8 What are two types of pollination?

9 What's the name of the process which plants use to make their own food?

10 What do plants release into the air?

Now look at units 1, 2, 3 and 4 and check your answers.

Listen and check your answers.

How did you do?

8–10 points	5–7 points	0–4 points
Excellent	Good	Try again

SCIENCE CHALLENGE

Find a friend. Decide who is Pupil A and who is Pupil B. Take it in turns to ask and answer the questions in the Science Challenge.

PUPIL A

1 The digestive system starts here.
2 The remains of the food that our body can't use leave our body here.
3 Urine collects here in the excretory system.
4 These blood vessels carry blood and nutrients from the heart to all parts of our body.
5 This system is made up of the organs that help us breathe.
6 This is what happens when a sperm joins an egg.
7 These vertebrates drink their mother's milk.
8 These vertebrates breathe through their gills.
9 This is the female reproductive organ of a flower.
10 The ovary of a flower produces these.

PUPIL B

1 Food travels down the oesophagus to this part of the digestive system.
2 These two small organs in the excretory system clean the waste from our blood.
3 These blood vessels carry blood back to the heart from the rest of our body.
4 These are very small blood vessels that connect our arteries and veins.
5 Amphibians change and grow into adults in this process.
6 The body of these invertebrates is divided into three parts and they have six legs.
7 These vertebrates lay eggs and have a beak.
8 These are the male reproductive organs of a flower.
9 The male reproductive organs of a flower produce this.
10 Fertilisation happens here in a plant.

Can you remember the definitions of these words?

break down *(verb)* ...
fertilisation *(noun)* ...
herbaceous plant *(noun)* ...
pollination *(noun)* ...
sucker *(noun)* ...
vessel *(noun)* ...

Answers on Photocopiable Resources CD, Unit 4.

In this unit, we're going to learn about our planet, the Earth.

The **solar system** is made up of all the planets that orbit **the Sun**. The Sun is a star. It's in the centre of the solar system.

Eight **planets** orbit the Sun. They're called **Mercury**, **Venus**, **Earth**, **Mars**, **Jupiter**, **Saturn**, **Uranus** and **Neptune**. The Earth is the third planet from the Sun and the moon is its satellite . The moon orbits the Earth. Some other planets have one or more satellites, but others have none. The Sun, the planets and satellites are all called **celestial bodies**. This means that they're natural objects in the sky.

orbit *(verb)* the way an object travels around a larger object in space.

satellite *(noun)* a celestial body that travels around a planet.

Do you know the names of all the planets in the solar system?

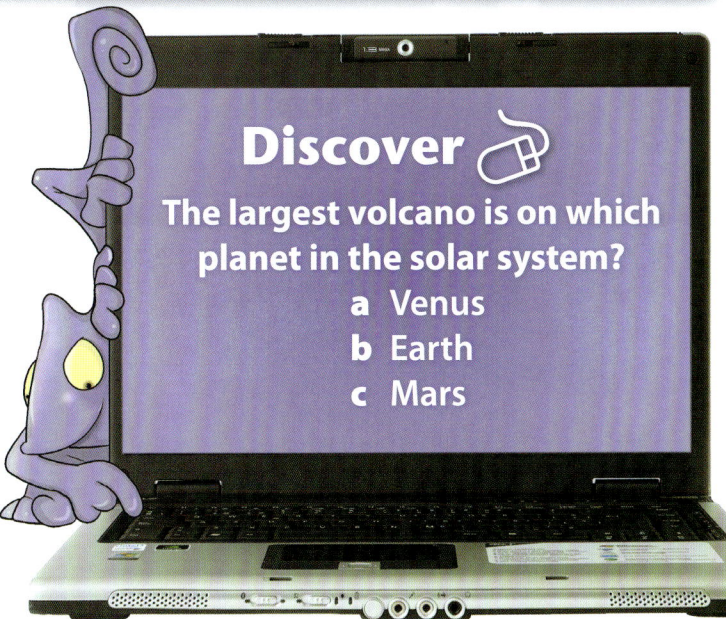

Discover

The largest volcano is on which planet in the solar system?

    a Venus
    b Earth
    c Mars

1  **Say the *Solar system* chant.**

2 **What is the solar system made up of?**

The solar system is made up of …

3 **Copy the picture of the solar system. Identify and label the Earth.**

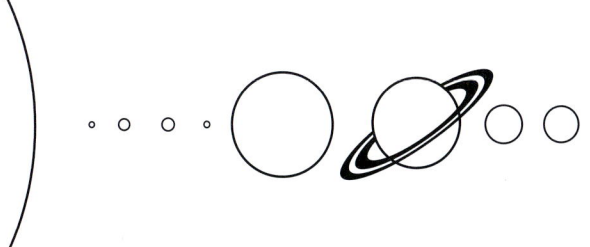

4 **Which is the biggest planet?**

5 **Which is the smallest planet?**

6 **Which do you think is the hottest planet? Why?**

*The hottest planet is …
because …*

7 **Which planet do you think takes the longest to orbit the Sun? Why?**

… takes the longest to orbit the Sun because …

8 **Which is the only star that we can see from the Earth during the day?**

9 **True or false? Copy the sentences and correct the ones that are false.**

  a Mercury is the nearest planet to the Sun.

  b Uranus is the furthest planet from the Sun.

  c The Sun is the Earth's satellite.

  d All the planets have satellites.

The Earth's moon

The **moon** is the Earth's only natural satellite. The moon takes about twenty-eight days to orbit the Earth and it rotates on its axis at the same time. The bright part of the moon is the part that the Sun is shining on. The moon reflects this light from the Sun and this is what we see from the Earth. The moon looks as if it's changing shape and we call these shapes the **phases of the moon**.

There are six main phases: **new moon**, **crescent moon**, **first quarter**, **full moon**, **third quarter** and **crescent moon**.

  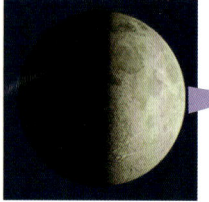  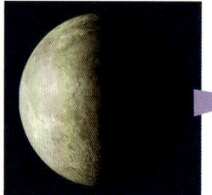

| new moon | crescent moon | first quarter | full moon | third quarter | crescent moon |

A **solar eclipse** happens when the moon passes between the Earth and the Sun and the Sun isn't visible from the Earth.

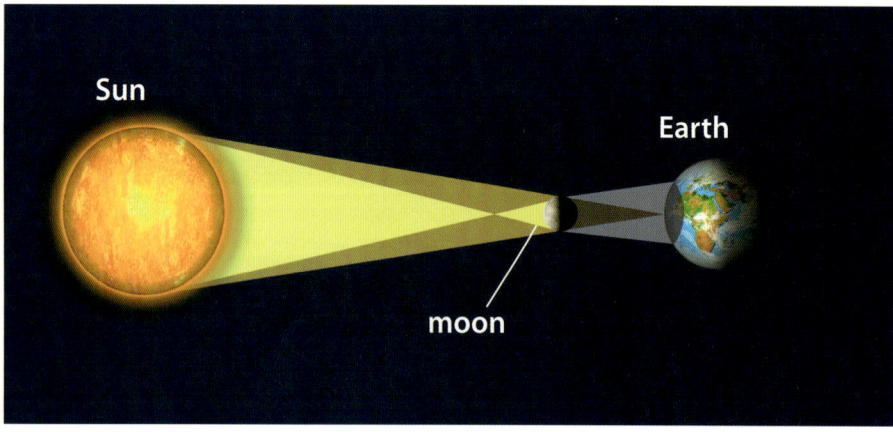

Sun
Earth
moon

1 **Why does the moon look as if it's changing shape?**

2 **What are the six main phases of the moon?**

3 Sing the *Moon* song.

4 **What phase of the moon can you see tonight?**

Tonight there's a . . .

The Earth rotates on its axis and this **rotation** is why we have **day and night**. It takes twenty-four hours to complete one rotation. The Sun shines on one half of the Earth, so it's day on the half of the Earth that faces the Sun. It's night on the half of the Earth that faces away from the Sun.

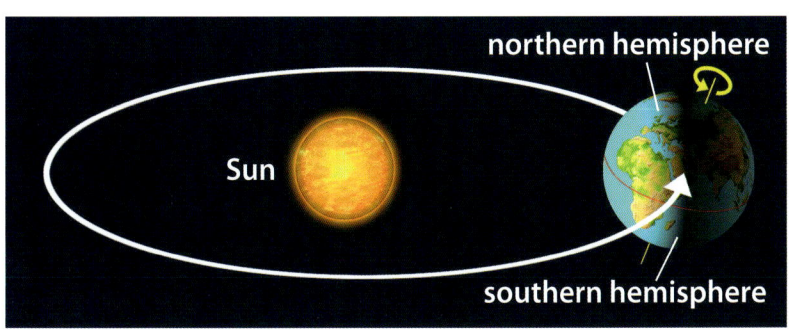

The **Earth's axis is tilted**. When the Earth orbits the Sun, one **hemisphere** receives more light and heat than the other. This causes different **climates** on Earth and different seasons.

When it's winter in the **northern hemisphere**, it's summer in the **southern hemisphere**. So when it's winter in Spain, it's summer in Australia!

Let's investigate! — The Earth's orbit

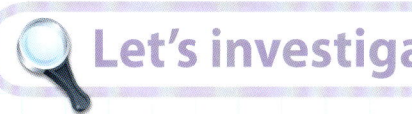

Investigate how the Earth orbits the Sun.

You need:
- a large ball
- an orange
- a pen
- a knitting needle

Why does the Earth have different seasons?

a Rotate the Earth on its axis and move it around the Sun.

1 **How long does it take the Earth to complete one rotation?**

It takes the Earth …

2 **How long do you think it takes the Earth to orbit the Sun?**

3 **Me** **Is Spain in the northern or the southern hemisphere?**

4 **When it's winter in the northern hemisphere, what season is it in the southern hemisphere?**

Our planet

We use **maps** and **globes** to show the Earth. Maps show the Earth as flat. Globes show the Earth as a ⬚ sphere ⬚. Globes also show how the Earth is tilted on its axis.

The Earth's axis goes through the North Pole to the South Pole. The Earth rotates on its axis.

The **Equator** is a line that goes horizontally around the Earth. This line divides the Earth into the northern hemisphere and the southern hemisphere.

Lines of latitude go horizontally around the Earth. We use these lines to measure distance from the Equator.

Lines of longitude go vertically around the Earth from the North Pole to the South Pole. We use these lines to measure how far east or west a place is.

sphere *(noun)* an object that is round like a ball.

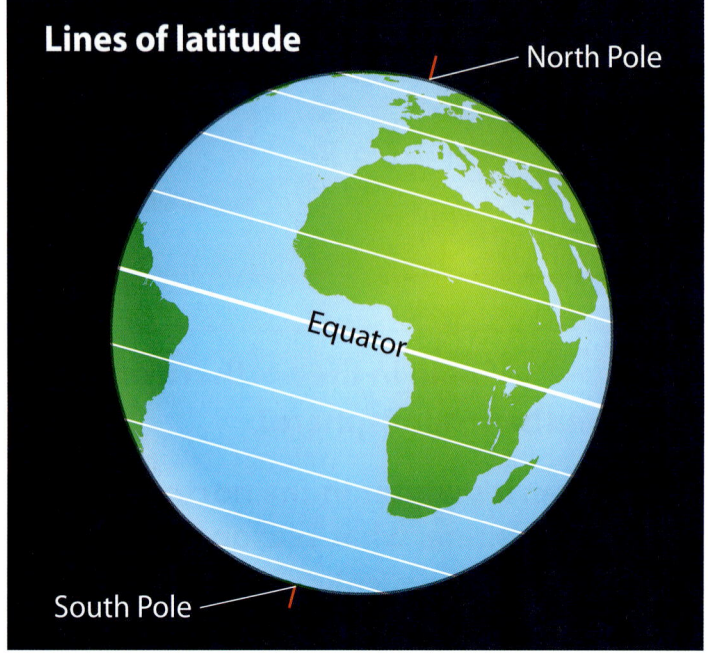

Lines of latitude

North Pole

Equator

South Pole

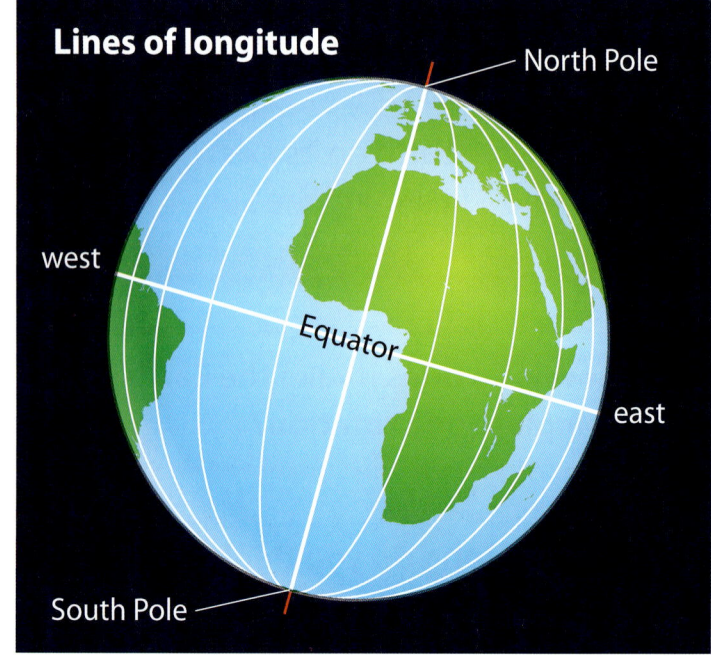

Lines of longitude

North Pole

west

Equator

east

South Pole

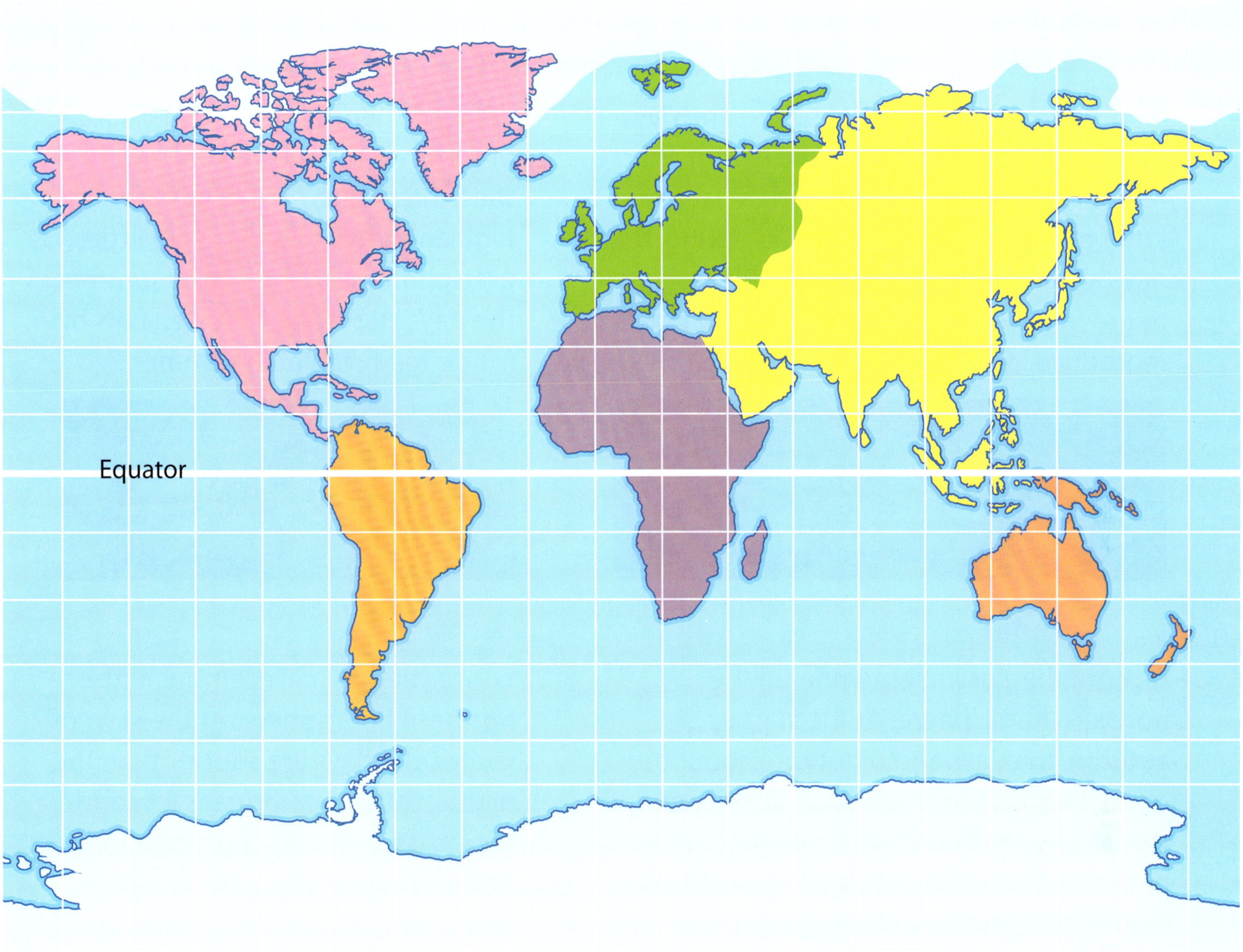

Equator

1  **Is Spain north or south of the Equator?**

2 **Can you name a country in the southern hemisphere?**

3 **What are the differences between globes and maps?**

4 **What are the advantages and disadvantages of globes and maps?**

5 **Copy and complete the sentences.**

   a Lines of   go horizontally around the Earth.

   b Lines of   go vertically around the Earth.

DID YOU KNOW?

The Earth is sometimes called the 'blue planet'. Do you know why?

Spring begins in March in the northern hemisphere. At the start of spring, the days and nights are about the same length, the temperature increases and there's usually a lot of precipitation. At the end of spring, the days are longer than the nights. Plants start to grow flowers and fruit and many animals reproduce in spring.

Summer begins in June in the northern hemisphere. At the start of summer, the days are longer than the nights, the temperature is high and there's usually very little precipitation. At the end of summer, the days start to get shorter. Lots of fruit is ready to eat in summer.

Autumn begins in September in the northern hemisphere. At the start of autumn, the days and nights are about the same length, the temperature decreases and there's usually a lot of precipitation. At the end of autumn, the days are shorter than the nights. Deciduous trees start to lose their leaves and many animals collect food for winter.

Winter begins in December in the northern hemisphere. At the start of winter, the days are shorter than the nights, the temperature is low and there's usually some precipitation. At the end of winter, the days start to get longer. Deciduous trees lose their leaves in winter and many animals hibernate.

1 **Which season has the longest days?**

2 **Which season has the longest nights?**

3 **When do the different seasons begin in the northern hemisphere?**

4 **Me** **What's your favourite season? Why?**

My favourite season is … because …

Climate is the usual weather in a place over a long period of time. Climates on Earth can be hot, cold, humid or dry. Climate is influenced by latitude. The places nearer the Equator have higher temperatures and more precipitation.

Different plants and animals live in different climates.

Climate isn't the same as weather. Can you remember a definition for weather?

This area has an **Atlantic climate**. The temperature is mild in summer and it's cool in winter. There's a lot of precipitation all year.

This area has a **continental climate**. The temperature is very high in summer and it's very low in winter. There's little precipitation, but there can be storms in summer.

Las Islas Canarias have a **sub-tropical climate**. The temperature is high in summer and this changes little during other seasons. There's very little precipitation.

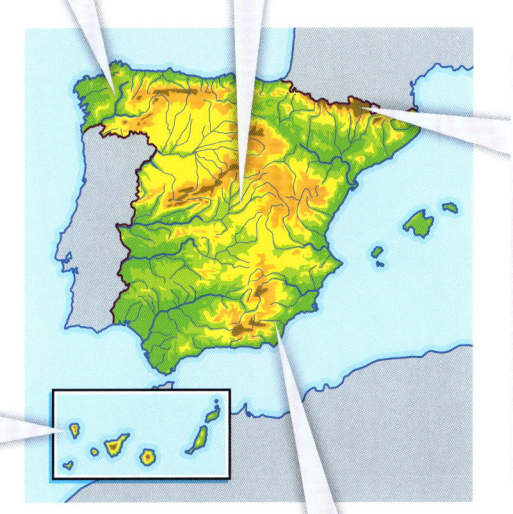

Mountain areas have a **mountain climate**. It's cool in summer and the temperature is very low in winter. There's a lot of precipitation all year and this falls as snow in winter.

This area has a **Mediterranean climate**. The temperature is high in summer and it's mild during other seasons. There can be a lot of precipitation in autumn, but there's very little precipitation during other seasons.

1 What's the difference between weather and climate?

2 Say the *Climates* chant.

3 What are the characteristics of the climate in your area?

The solar eclipse

1. Something amazing is happening today.

Look at all the people looking at the sky.

2. Look!

3. This is incredible!

4. The Sun is going to disappear.

… but it's midday.

5. Now I can't see the Sun.

And I can't see anything. It's dark.

6. Now I can see a bit of the Sun again.

7. This is amazing!

We're so lucky to see a solar eclipse.

A **solar eclipse** only happens during a new moon. A solar eclipse happens when **the moon passes between the Earth and the Sun** and blocks the light from the Sun. During a total eclipse, all we can see is a ring of light around the moon. Total eclipses don't happen very often and most people are very lucky if they see just one eclipse.

It's very dangerous to look at a solar eclipse without special protection for your eyes, and remember not to look directly at the Sun.

THE CLIMATE WHERE I LIVE

1 🌟Me **Write a text about the climate where you live.**

a What's the temperature like during the year?

b What's the precipitation like during the year?

c What plants and animals are there near you?

d How are these plants and animals adapted to the climate?

e How do you adapt to the climate during the year?

2 **Take photos or draw pictures to illustrate your text.**

REMEMBER!
There's no precipitation.
There are palm trees.

I live in Las Islas Canarias. The climate is a sub-tropical climate.

The temperature is high in summer and it can be warm during other seasons, too.

There's usually no precipitation in summer, but there's a little precipitation in spring, autumn and winter.

There are lots of palm trees and plants that don't need a lot of water. There are also irrigated crops like bananas.

There are lizards in Las Islas Canarias. Lizards are cold-blooded reptiles and need the heat of the Sun for warmth.

In summer, I wear shorts and t-shirts. I usually go to the beach, but I sometimes go to the beach in spring and autumn, too. In winter I wear trousers and jumpers.

1 **Copy and complete the word maps.**

Mars   Mercury   Neptune   third quarter   new moon   full moon   Saturn

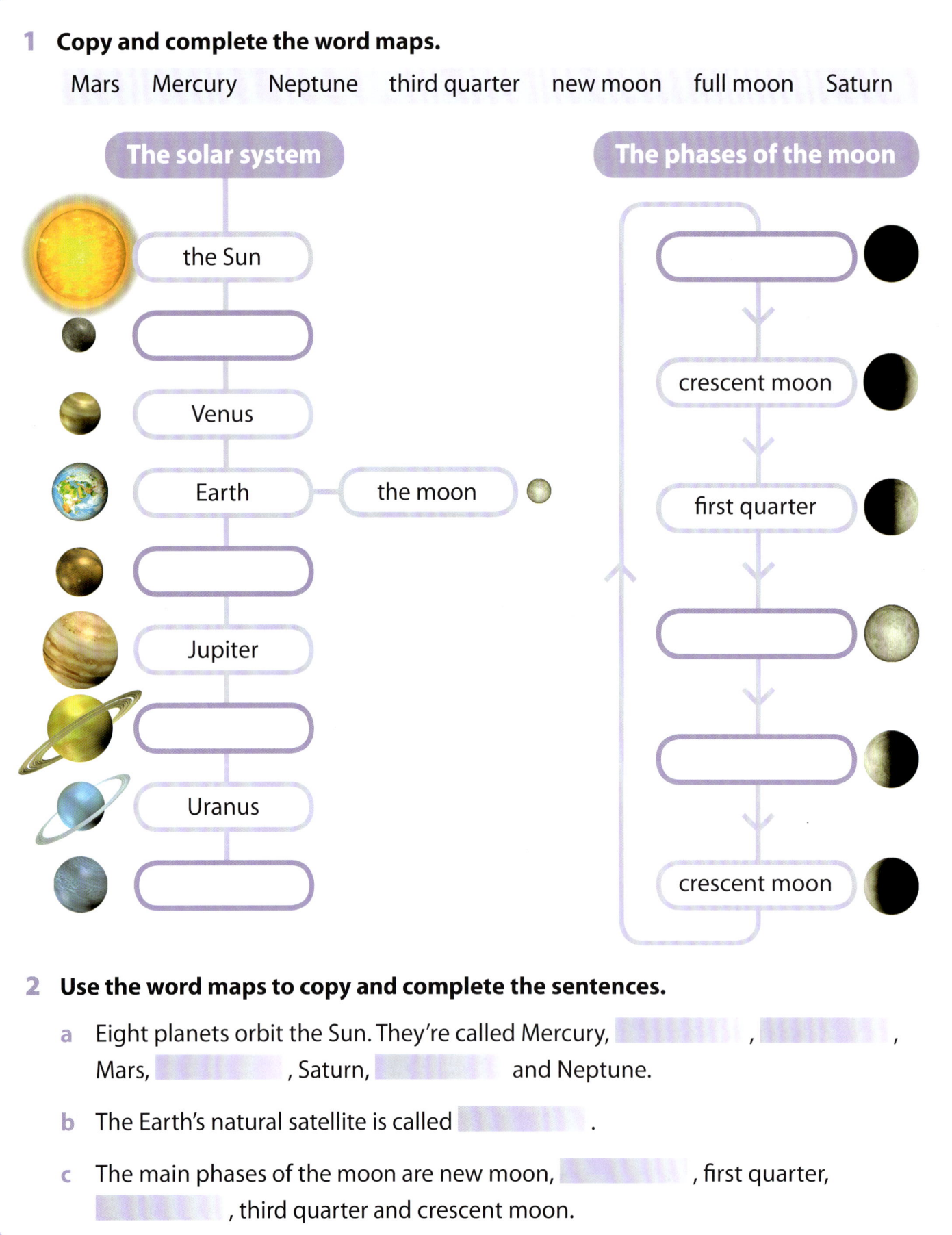

The solar system

the Sun

Venus

Earth — the moon

Jupiter

Uranus

The phases of the moon

crescent moon

first quarter

crescent moon

2 **Use the word maps to copy and complete the sentences.**

a Eight planets orbit the Sun. They're called Mercury, ⬚⬚⬚⬚⬚, ⬚⬚⬚⬚⬚, Mars, ⬚⬚⬚⬚⬚, Saturn, ⬚⬚⬚⬚⬚ and Neptune.

b The Earth's natural satellite is called ⬚⬚⬚⬚⬚ .

c The main phases of the moon are new moon, ⬚⬚⬚⬚⬚, first quarter, ⬚⬚⬚⬚⬚, third quarter and crescent moon.

3　**Copy and label the diagram of the Earth.**

Equator　　northern hemisphere　　southern hemisphere
lines of latitude　　lines of longitude

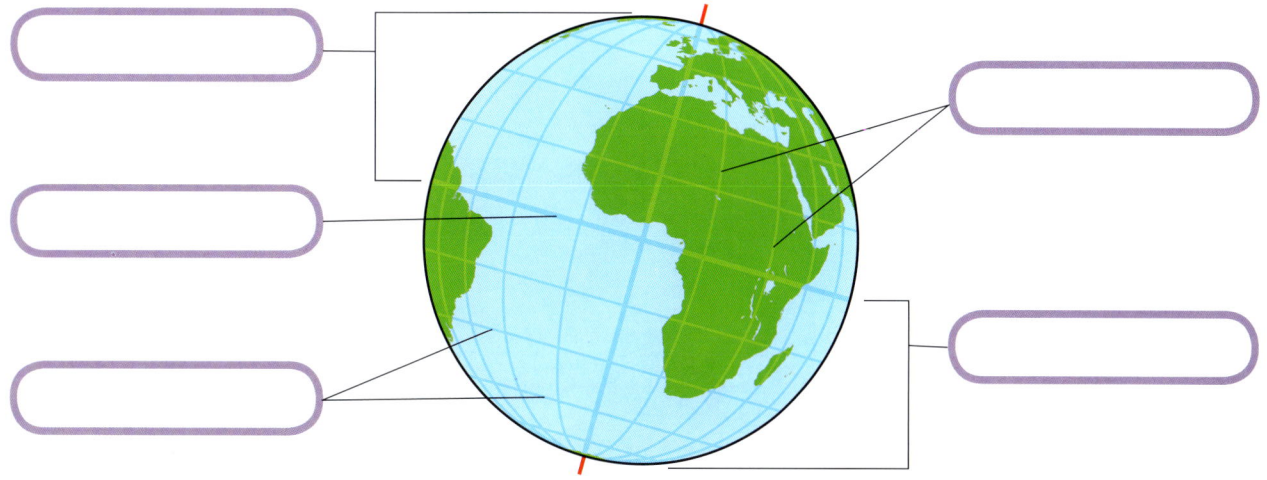

4　**Copy and correct the sentences.**

a　The **Equator** / **Earth's axis** divides the Earth into the northern hemisphere
and the southern hemisphere.

b　Lines of latitude go **horizontally** / **vertically** around the Earth.

c　Lines of longitude go **horizontally** / **vertically** around the Earth from the
North Pole to the South Pole.

d　It takes the Earth **twenty-four hours** / **one year** to orbit the Sun.

e　Summer begins in **June** / **December** in the northern hemisphere.

f　In an Atlantic climate there is **a lot of** / **little** precipitation all year.

 I can identify celestial bodies in the solar system.　　☆ ☆ ☆

I know the characteristics and phases of the moon.　　☆ ☆ ☆

I understand the Earth's rotation and orbit.　　☆ ☆ ☆

I can identify and describe different climates in Spain.　　☆ ☆ ☆

In this unit, we're going to learn about different forms of energy and sources of energy.

We can change energy from one form to another, but we can't make it disappear.

Energy is important for everything we do. Energy has different forms.

Thermal energy is in anything that's hot. The Sun produces lots of thermal energy.

The Sun produces lots of **light energy**, too. Plants need light energy to grow.

Anything that makes a noise has **sound energy**. A vibrating drum is an example of sound energy.

We use **electrical energy** for a lot of things in our homes. Lightning also produces electrical energy.

Food contains **chemical energy**. Our body turns the energy into heat or kinetic energy. Fuels like wood also contain chemical energy.

Moving things have **kinetic energy**. These moving things can be big like planets, or small like insects. When we ride a bike, we turn the chemical energy from the food we eat into kinetic energy.

1 Say the *Energy* chant.

2 **Look at the picture. What forms of energy can you identify?**

3 **Listen to Clara and Yousef talking about energy.**

4 **Identify the forms of energy in photos a–c.**

a   b   c

🔍 **Investigate thermal energy.**

You need:
- a glass of cold water
- a glass of hot water
- food colouring

Do hot things contain more energy than cold things?

a Put three drops of food colouring in each glass of water and wait.

b Predict which water will change colour most quickly.

HOT COLD

c Discuss the results.
1 Did the hot water or the cold water change colour the quickest?
2 Results: **Cold** / **Hot** water contains more energy.

Light is a form of energy. Light sources are things that produce light; they can be natural like the Sun, or man-made like light bulbs and candles.

We need light to see. If it's dark, we can't see anything.

Light always travels in a straight line. It can't move around objects.

Light travels in all directions.

Light is the fastest form of energy. When we switch on a light in a room, we see it immediately. The Sun is millions of kilometres away from the Earth, but it only takes about eight minutes for sunlight to reach us because light travels at about 300 000 km per second.

The light from the Sun looks white, but it's made up of seven different colours: red, orange, yellow, green, blue, indigo and violet. We can see these seven colours in a rainbow in the sky.

1 **What man-made sources of light can you name?**

. . . is a man-made source of light.

2 **What sources of light do you use? Why?**

I use . . . to . . .

3 **Is light really white?**

DID YOU KNOW?

Some nocturnal insects, like the firefly, produce their own light. A few deep sea fish, like the lantern fish, produce light, too.

When light reaches an object, it can do one or more of the following things: it can be **reflected**, it can be **absorbed** or it can **pass through** the object.

Investigate what happens when light reaches an object.

You need:
- a torch
- black card
- tissue paper
- a mirror

How does light interact with an object?

a Shine the torch on the objects. What happens to the light?

①

②

b Discus the results and copy and complete the sentences.

1 When light shines on black card, it _____ .

2 When light shines on tissue paper, it _____ .

3 When light shines on a mirror, it _____ .

③

 Investigate how shadows change during the day.

> Why do shadows change shape?

You need:
- a stick
- a ruler
- a compass

a Stand the stick in a sunny place.
b Measure the shadow.
c Record the position of the Sun.
d Record the position of the shadow.
e Discuss the results. Copy and complete the chart.

	Morning	Midday	Afternoon
Length of shadow (cm)			
Position of the Sun			
Position of shadow			

> When light hits an opaque object, a shadow forms on the **opposite** side of the object.

1 Order pictures a–d to show how shadows change during the day.

a

b

c

d

Sound

Sound is produced when objects **vibrate**. Sound travels in **waves** and in **all directions**. It also travels **very fast**, but it travels nowhere near as fast as light. Loud sounds travel further than quiet sounds, and a sound is always louder nearer its source.

Sound can travel through **air** and **water** and, unlike light, sound can travel through **solid**, **opaque objects**.

Sound can't travel when there's no air. This means there's no sound in space or on the moon.

Sound travels in **all directions**.

Sound can travel **through water**.

Sound can travel **through solid objects**.

Sound, like light, can also **reflect** off some objects. When this happens, we can hear an **echo**.

1 How is sound produced?

2 Compare the characteristics of light and sound.

3 Sing the *Light and sound* song.

4 Why do we see lightning before we hear thunder in a storm?

We see lightning first because ...

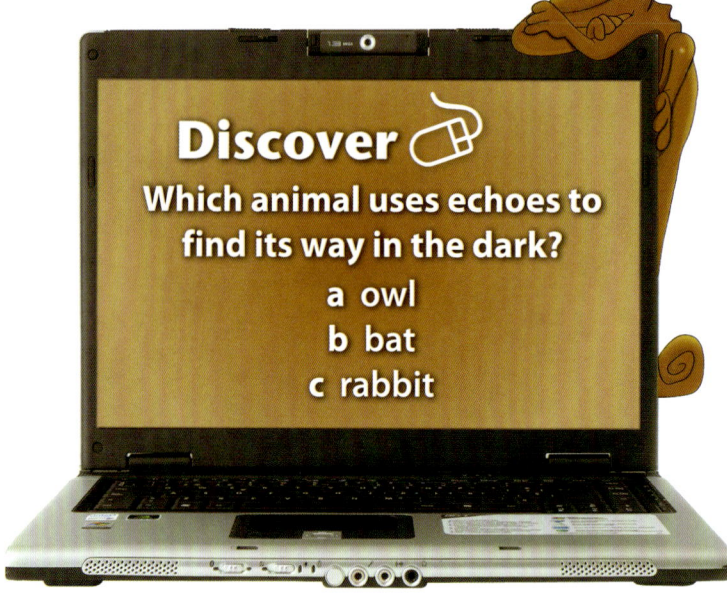

Discover
Which animal uses echoes to find its way in the dark?
a owl
b bat
c rabbit

Renewable and non-renewable energy sources

Energy can be obtained from **renewable** or **non-renewable** sources. Most of our electricity comes from power stations that use energy sources like **coal**, **oil** and **gas** to make electricity. These are non-renewable energy sources. This means that we can't make more of them and they'll eventually run out .

We can also get energy from **the Sun**, **wind** and **water**. These are renewable energy sources. This means that we can use them again and again and they'll never run out.

run out *(verb)* to use all of something and have nothing left.

Using non-renewable energy sources causes **pollution** and can harm the environment.

Renewable energy sources cause less pollution. What energy sources do you use at home? Can you remember how to save energy?

DID YOU KNOW?

Coal, oil and gas are called fossil fuels. This is because they take millions of years to form.

1 Copy and write the correct sentences.

a A non-renewable energy source will **eventually run out** / **never run out**.

b A renewable energy source will **eventually run out** / **never run out**.

2 Identify the energy sources in photos a–d. Are they renewable or non-renewable sources?

3 Can you think of any disadvantages of renewable energy sources?

a

b

c

d

The world of mirrors

1
Look, there's a fair.
Let's go in.

2
The world of mirrors
What's that? The world of mirrors …

3
I'm tall and thin.
And I'm short and fat!

4
My neck is so long.
You look like a giraffe.

5
Look! That man's legs are so long.
And that man is very fat. Mirrors can be very funny.

6
Erm … They aren't using mirrors. They're clowns.

Most **mirrors** are made of a sheet of **polished glass** with a thin coat of **silver paint** on the back. The silver reflects the light. When we look in a mirror, we see ourselves because the light is reflected from us to the mirror, and then back from the mirror to our eyes.

Ordinary mirrors are flat, and we see a true image of ourselves. Some mirrors are curved and wavy. These mirrors reflect the light in different directions, so that we look taller and thinner, shorter and fatter, or we have a much longer neck!

HOW I USE ENERGY

1 ⭐Me **Write a text about the forms of energy you use.**

a What forms of energy do you use every day?

b How do you use these forms of energy?

c Identify the sources of some of these forms of energy.

d Are these energy sources renewable or non-renewable?

e ♻ How do you save energy?

2 **Find photos or draw pictures to illustrate your text.**

REMEMBER!

I use kinetic energy to ride my bike.

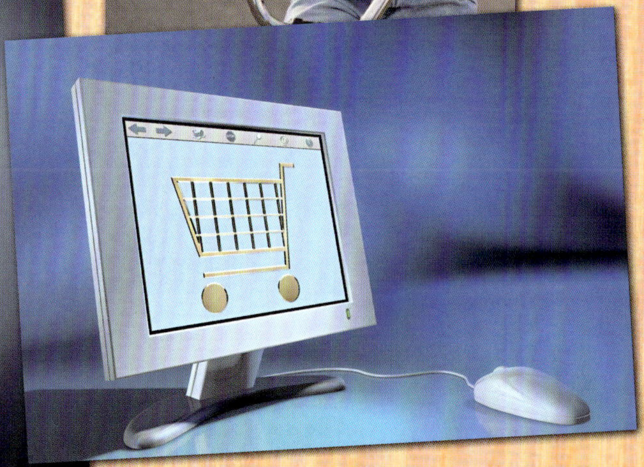

I use lots of different forms of energy every day.
I use kinetic energy to ride my bike, ...
I get kinetic energy from chemical energy in my food.

Learning to learn

1 **Copy and complete the word maps.**

electrical   coal   light   wind   kinetic   sound

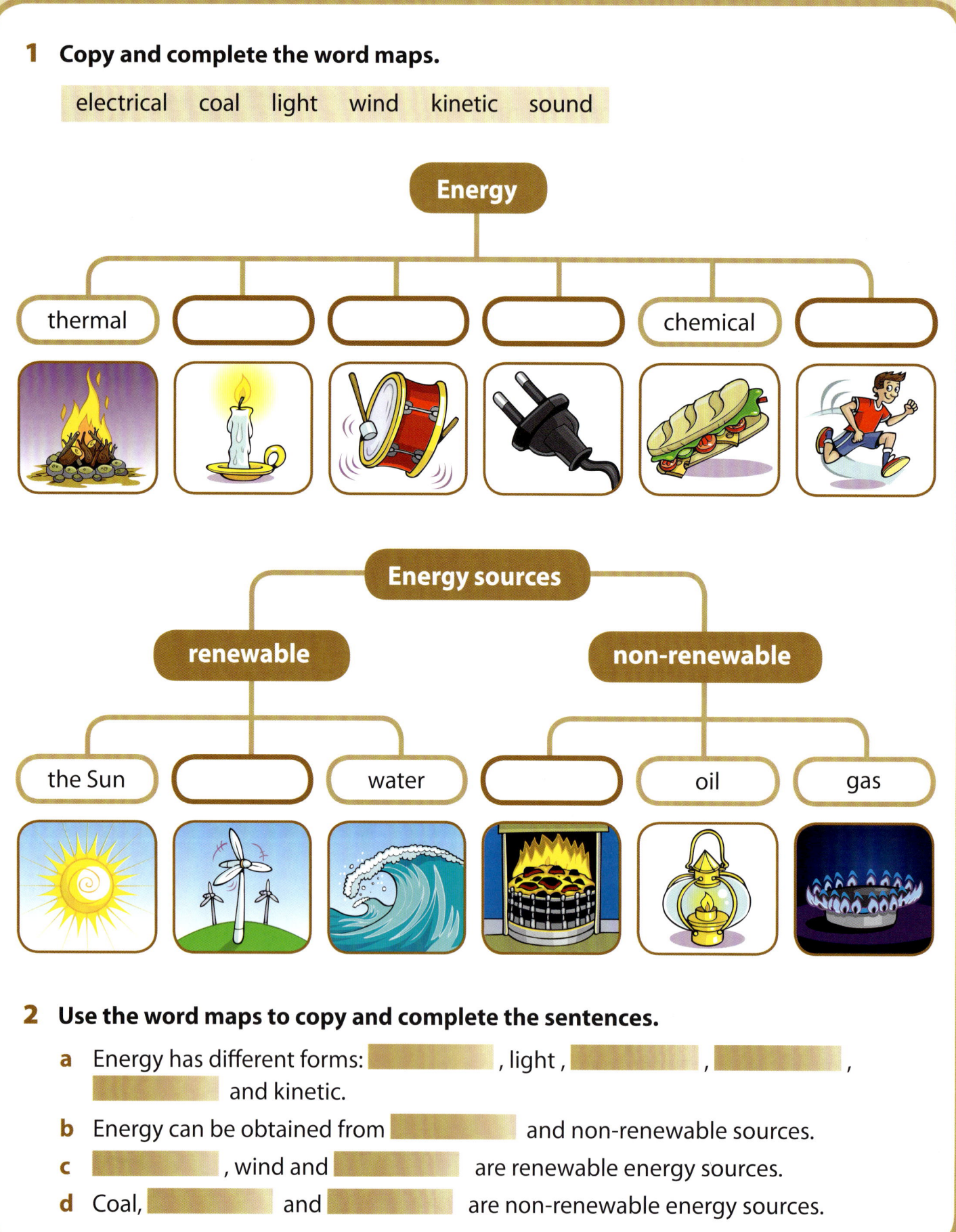

2 **Use the word maps to copy and complete the sentences.**

a Energy has different forms: ▬▬▬▬▬ , light , ▬▬▬▬▬ , ▬▬▬▬▬ , ▬▬▬▬▬ and kinetic.

b Energy can be obtained from ▬▬▬▬▬ and non-renewable sources.

c ▬▬▬▬▬ , wind and ▬▬▬▬▬ are renewable energy sources.

d Coal, ▬▬▬▬▬ and ▬▬▬▬▬ are non-renewable energy sources.

3 **True or false? Copy the sentences and correct the ones that are false.**

  a Light always travels in a straight line.

  b Light travels in all directions.

  c Light is the slowest form of energy.

4 **Copy the picture and draw the shadow of the tree. Is it morning or afternoon?**

5 **Copy the chart and classify the energy sources.**

oil   wind   gas   coal   the Sun   water

Renewable	Non-renewable

6 **Copy and complete the sentences.**

  a _____ energy sources will eventually run out.

  b _____ energy sources will never run out.

I know some different forms of energy.

I know the characteristics of light.

I know the characteristics of sound.

I can identify some sources of energy.

I know the differences between renewable and non-renewable energy sources.

We need machines

In this unit we're going to learn about simple and complex machines.

How many of these simple and complex machines can you name?

A **machine** is something we use to make work easier. We can classify machines as **simple machines** or **complex machines**. Simple machines have few or no moving parts. When we put simple machines together we get a complex machine. All machines use energy, but many complex machines need electrical energy to work.

DID YOU KNOW?

The Ancient Egyptians used simple machines to build the pyramids!

1 **Look at the picture and identify the machines.**

2 **What are the differences between simple machines and complex machines?**

3 **Copy the chart and classify the machines in the picture.**

Simple machines	Complex machines

4 **Listen to Nico and Yousef talking about machines.**

5 **Identify the machines in the picture that need electrical energy to work.**

Simple machines

There are six simple machines:

1

A **pulley** uses a wheel and a rope to lift or lower an object.

2

An **inclined plane** is a slanting surface that connects a low level with a high level. We use it to move objects up or down.

3

A **screw** is a type of inclined plane. We use it to hold things together or lift objects.

4

A **wheel** is a circular object that turns around an **axle**. We use it to lift or move objects.

5

A **wedge** is an object with at least one slanting edge. We use it to cut objects.

6

A **lever** is a rigid bar with a support called a **fulcrum**. We use it to lift or move objects.

Remember, machines can be dangerous! It's important to use machines properly and ask an adult for help if you need it!

1 Say the *Simple machines* chant.

2 **Copy and complete the sentences.**

a A ▭ is an object with at least one slanting edge. We use it to cut objects.

b A ▭ is a circular object that turns around an ▭ . We use it to lift or move objects.

c A ▭ is a rigid bar with a support called a ▭ . We use it to lift or move objects.

d An ▭ is a slanting surface that connects a low level with a high level. We use it to move objects up or down.

e A ▭ is a type of inclined plane. We use it to hold things together or lift objects.

f A ▭ uses a wheel and a rope to lift or lower an object.

3 Say the *Simple machines* rap.

4 **Identify the simple machines in pictures a–f.**

5 **Can you think of any more examples of simple machines?**

a **b**

c **d**

e **f**

Discover

Which two simple machines are used to make a pencil sharpener?

a a wheel and an axle
b a lever and a wedge
c a screw and a wedge

Investigate pulleys.

You need:
- a coat hanger
- a cotton reel
- string

How does a pulley work?

a Make a pulley.

b Lift an object without using the pulley.

c Lift the same object using the pulley.

d Discuss the results.

   1 What objects can you lift with your pulley?

   2 A pulley makes the objects feel **lighter** / **heavier**.

Complex machines

What complex machines can you see in your classroom?

Complex machines are made up of a number of simple machines working together. Complex machines need **energy** to work. This energy can come from **people**, **electricity** or **fuel**. We use complex machines every day. They're in our homes, in our school, in the towns and cities where we live, and they're also used to help people at work.

- Electrical appliances in our homes such as washing machines and cookers use electricity from the mains and calculators at school use electricity from batteries.

- Forms of transport such as cars, buses and lorries use fuels like petrol and diesel to work. Bicycles use energy from people.

- At work we use robots to make mass-produced products. Robots can be quicker than people and they can do jobs that are dangerous for people.

Machines are improving all the time. They're getting quicker, more efficient and safer to use.

> **efficient** *(adj)* something that works very well and doesn't waste energy.

1 Look at pictures a–e.

a Where can you see these complex machines?

b What forms of energy do these complex machines use?

c Me Which of these complex machines do you use?

2 Can you think of any disadvantages of using robots at work?

3 Match and write the sentences.

a We use a washing machine   to cook food.

b We use a cooker   to travel from one place to another.

c We use a bicycle   to wash clothes.

d We use a robot   to help us do maths.

e We use a calculator   to make mass-produced products.

How a complex machine works

CD2 35

Remember to wear a helmet when you ride a bicycle!

A **bicycle** is a complex machine that's made up of simple machines. A bicycle needs our kinetic energy to work.

We hold the **handlebars** and use these to change direction. The handlebars are levers.

The **pedals** are levers, too. We push the pedals with our feet, and when the pedals turn around, the wheels of the bicycle turn around, too.

gear controls
handlebars
brake levers
brakes
gears
tyre
pedal
front wheel
back wheel

When we want to go up or down a hill, we use our hands to change the **gear controls**. The **gears** are pulleys and the force travels along the chain to the back wheel.

When we want to stop the bicycle, we use our hands to push and pull the **brake levers**. This force travels along cables to the **brakes**. The brakes press against the wheels and this force slows the speed of the bicycle.

1 **Look at the photos below. Identify the parts of the bicycle a–e.**

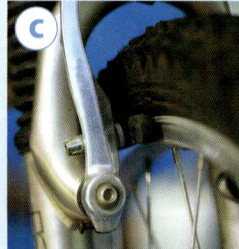

2 **Copy and match the definitions.**

  a brakes   These are levers. We push them with our feet. They make the wheels turn around.

  b handlebars   These press against the wheels to slow the speed of the bicycle.

  c gears   These are pulleys. The force from them travels along the chain to the back wheel.

  d pedals   These are levers. We use them to change direction when we're on a bicycle.

3 **Read about how bicycles have changed over time. Match the texts to the pictures.**

We already know that machines are always changing and getting quicker, more efficient and safer to use. Let's learn about how the bicycle has changed over time.

1   The first bicycles were made of wood. They had no pedals and people sat on the seat and used their feet to walk at the same time.

2   Then, a bicycle with pedals was invented. This bicycle was made of wood and later had metal tyres. It was very uncomfortable!

3   Next, a bicycle with a very big front wheel was invented. This bicycle was made of metal and its tyres were made of solid rubber. It could be dangerous to ride!

4   After this, both wheels were the same size again, but the wheels were still made of solid rubber.

5   Finally, the first bicycle with air in its tyres was invented. Today, bicycles are faster, more comfortable and much safer.

Great inventions can be very simple, like the wheel, or more complex, like the bicycle.

Anyone can be an inventor. What can you invent to make your life better?

The Science Fair

1
Can we go to the Science Fair?

Yes, but first we need a Science project.

Let's build a machine.

School Science fair at the Science Museum

2
We need wheels, ...

3
... screws and an old box, ...

4
... and a big fan.

5
This machine uses energy from the wind.

Science Club

We use it for Science Club trips.

6
It carries our food, water and books.

This means that we can save our energy.

7
And the winner of the machine that uses renewable energy is the Science Club!

A **robot** is a machine that can do work automatically. This means that it can do things on its own without thinking. Robots use electricity and can be controlled by people using computers. Robots can be any shape or size. We use robots in factories and to do dangerous jobs. There are robots in space, too! We send robots to other planets to investigate soil, rocks and the atmosphere and the robots send information back to Earth.

AN IMPORTANT INVENTION

1 **Write a text about an important invention.**

   a Find out when it was first invented and who invented it.

   b Describe how this invention has changed over time.

   c Why do you think this invention is important?

   d Can you think of ways to improve this invention?

2 **Find photos or draw pictures to illustrate your text.**

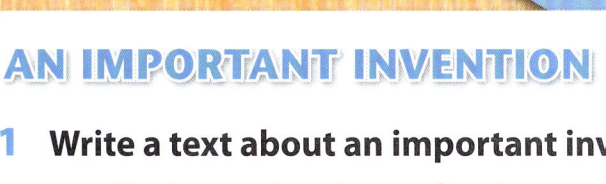

REMEMBER!

It was invented in ...
It was invented by ...

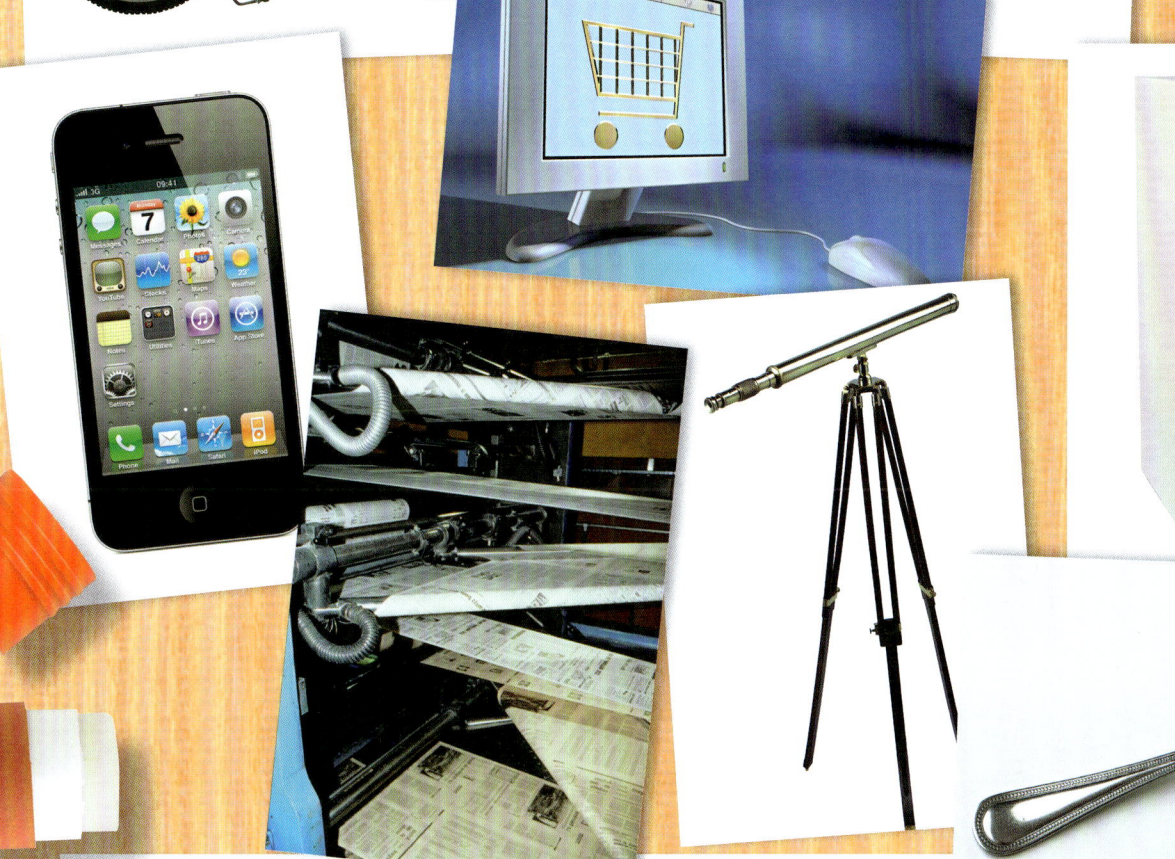

I think the most important invention is ...
It was invented in ... by ...
When it was first invented it was ... Now it's ...
I think this invention is important because ...

1 **Copy and complete the word maps.**

robot   screw   washing machine   pulley   calculator   lever   wheel and axle

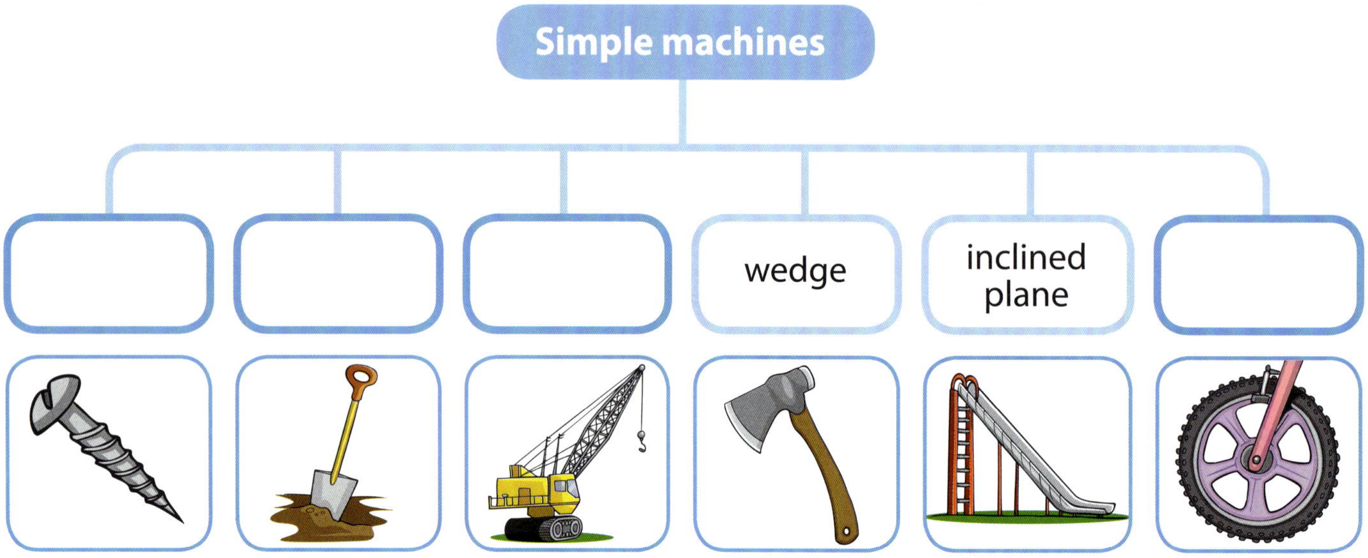

Simple machines

| | | | wedge | inclined plane | |

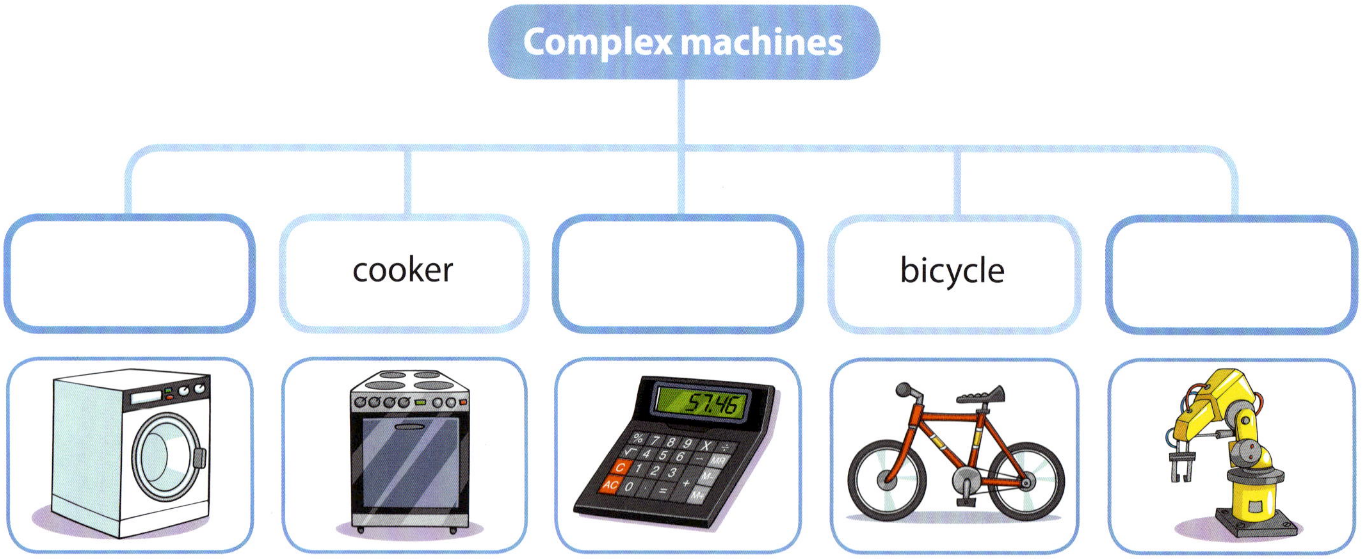

Complex machines

| | cooker | | bicycle | |

2 **Use the word maps to copy and complete the sentences.**

a ▢▢▢▢▢▢ have few or no moving parts. When you put simple machines together you get a ▢▢▢▢▢▢ .

b There are six simple machines: the screw, the ▢▢▢▢▢▢ , the pulley, the ▢▢▢▢▢▢ , the ▢▢▢▢▢▢ , and the wheel and axle .

3 **Look at the picture. Which simple machines can you use to do the following?**

  a Lift the box to the window.

  b Cut the rope around the box.

  c Open the lid of the box.

4 **Copy and complete the sentences.**

I can use a ▓▓▓▓▓ to lift the box to the window. I can use a ▓▓▓▓▓ to cut the rope around the box. I can use a ▓▓▓▓▓ to open the lid of the box.

5 **Copy the definitions and write the names of the complex machines.**

  a We use this to make mass-produced products.

  b We use this to cook food.

  c We use this to wash clothes.

  d We use this to help us do maths.

  e We use this to travel from one place to another.

6 **Read the definitions and copy and label the parts of the bicycle.**

  a We use these levers to change direction.

  b We push these levers with our feet.

  c The force from these pulleys travels along the chain to the back wheel.

  d These press against the wheels to slow the speed of the bicycle.

I can identify different simple machines. ☆ ☆ ☆

I can identify the parts of some complex machines. ☆ ☆ ☆

I know how we use some simple and complex machines. ☆ ☆ ☆

I know about some important inventions and how machines change over time. ☆ ☆ ☆

In this unit we're going to learn about matter and the properties of materials.

Can you describe any of these materials?

We already know that a table is made of wood, a pen is made of plastic and clothes are made of fabric, but what are all these things made up of? They are all made up of matter. **Matter** is all around us. Everything on Earth, and even everything in the solar system, is made up of matter. We're made up of matter, too! Matter is everything that we see, touch, taste or smell that has mass and volume .

mass *(noun)* how much matter an object has. We can measure mass in grams and kilograms.

volume *(noun)* the amount of space that matter takes up.

The three states of matter are **solid**, **liquid** and **gas**.

Solids have a definite shape. This means that when we put a solid in a different container, the shape of the solid doesn't change. Solids also **have a definite volume**, which means that a solid object always takes up the same amount of space. If we put a banana in a different container, it still has the same shape and the same volume.

Liquids don't have a definite shape. This means that they take on the shape of the container that they're in. Liquids do, however, **have a definite volume**. If we put some orange juice in a different container, it changes shape, but it still has the same volume.

Gases don't have a definite shape. Like liquids, the shape of a gas changes with the shape of its container. But unlike liquids and solids, gases expand to fill the container that they're in. This means that gases **don't have a definite volume**. For example, the shape and volume of air in balloons changes in different balloons.

expand *(verb)* to get larger in size or volume.

1 **Look at the picture and identify the solids, liquids and gases.**

2 **Listen to Nico, Clara and Yousef talking about matter.**

3 **Can you think of more examples of solids, liquids and gases?**

4 **Copy the chart and complete with a tick (✓) or a cross (✗). Write sentences.**

	Solids	Liquids	Gases
Have a definite shape			
Have a definite volume			

Changes in matter

Matter has three forms: solid, liquid and gas. Matter can change shape and state and we call this a **physical change**. Physical changes happen to water in the water cycle. In the water cycle, the water **changes shape** and **changes state**, but the **substance doesn't change**. This means that throughout the water cycle, the water stays as water.

Physical changes can happen when we **heat**, **freeze**, **bend**, **twist**, **stretch** or **squash** a substance.

A **chemical change** is when a **new substance is produced**. We can observe a chemical change when we cut an apple in half and leave it.

Chemical changes can happen when we **burn a substance** or **expose a substance to air**.

Let's investigate! — Chemical changes

 Observe a chemical change.

You need:
- an apple
- a knife

What chemical change can happen to an apple?

a   Cut the apple in half.

b   Wait 30 minutes.

c   Observe and describe what happens to the apple.

1   **What do we call water in its three forms?**

2   **Look at pictures a–d. Are these physical or chemical changes?**

3   **When can physical changes happen?**

Physical changes can happen when . . .

4   **When can chemical changes happen?**

5   **Say the *Changes in matter* rap.**

Most things around us are **mixtures**. A mixture is something that contains **two or more substances**.

We can find examples of mixtures in nature. Air is a mixture of gases. Saltwater in the sea is a mixture of water, salt and other minerals. Many rocks are a mixture of different minerals.

We can classify mixtures as **heterogeneous** or **homogeneous** mixtures. In a heterogeneous mixture it's easy to see the different substances. A fruit salad is a heterogeneous mixture. In a homogeneous mixture it isn't possible to see the different substances. Mayonnaise is a homogeneous mixture; it contains oil, eggs and vinegar, but we can't see these individual ingredients.

Let's investigate! — Separating mixtures

 Investigate separating mixtures.

You need:
- a clear container
- sand
- water

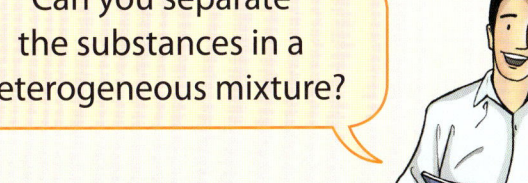
Can you separate the substances in a heterogeneous mixture?

a Make a mixture of sand and water.

b Can you separate this heterogeneous mixture?

c Discuss the results.

1 The substances in this heterogeneous mixture **can** / **can't** be separated.

2 Draw a picture and write a text to describe your results.

1 What are the differences between heterogeneous and homogeneous mixtures?

2 Copy the sentences and correct the ones that are false.

   a Air is a heterogeneous mixture.   **b** Saltwater is a homogeneous mixture.

3 Can you think of more examples of heterogeneous and homogeneous mixtures?

Let's investigate! **Mixtures**

🔍 **Investigate homogeneous and heterogeneous mixtures.**

You need:
- small spoons
- six clear containers
- water
- six different solids (coffee, white sugar, salt, chocolate powder, bread, small balls of plasticine)

What solids form a homogeneous mixture with water?

a Half fill a container with water.

b Add one spoon of coffee.

c Stir and observe if the solid dissolves in the water.

d Repeat the procedure with the different solids.

e Discuss the results.

1 Copy the chart and complete with a tick (✓) or a cross (✗).

Solid	Formed a heterogeneous mixture	Formed a homogeneous mixture
Coffee		
White sugar		
Salt		
Chocolate powder		
Bread		
Plasticine		

2 When the solid dissolves, a **heterogeneous** / **homogeneous** mixture is formed.

3 When the solid doesn't dissolve, a **heterogeneous** / **homogeneous** mixture is formed.

Properties of materials

Some materials are better for a purpose than others. This is because different materials have different **properties**.

A **resistant** material is difficult to break, but a **fragile** material breaks easily if we bend it or try to change its shape.

A **rigid** material doesn't bend easily, but we can bend a **flexible** material. An **elastic** material returns to its original shape after we bend or stretch it.

Some materials are **transparent**, which means that light can pass through them. When light can't pass through a material, we call the material **opaque**.

Some materials are **waterproof**, which means that water can't pass through them.

Heat passes through some materials easily and these materials are called **heat conductors**. Materials that heat can't pass through easily are called **heat insulators**.

DID YOU KNOW?

Diamond is the hardest natural material.

---

1 Say the *Properties of materials* chant.

2 Look at pictures a–j and identify the materials.

3 Identify the properties of these materials.

4 Why are pans usually made of metal with a handle made of wood or plastic?

5 Look around your classroom. Identify what materials objects are made of. Why are they made of these materials?

Natural and manufactured materials

CD2 49

We can classify materials into **natural materials** and **manufactured materials**.

Natural materials come from nature and can come from **plants**, **animals** or **minerals**. Wood, cotton and natural rubber come from plants. Wool, leather and silk come from animals, and rocks and oil come from minerals.

Manufactured materials are made from natural materials which are **transformed in a manufacturing process**. We manufacture glass from sand, and we use oil to make plastic, crayons and fabrics such as nylon.

a b c d

CD2 50

How paper is manufactured

 ①  ② 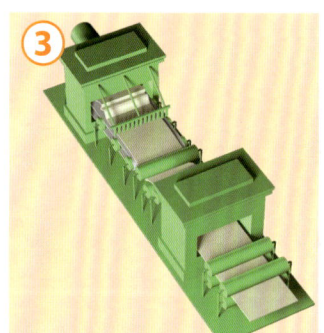 ③ 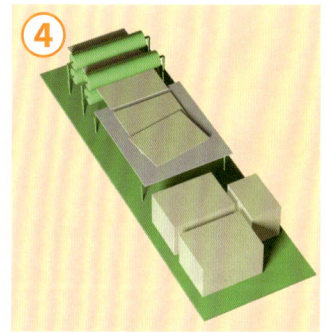 ④

1 **Read the definitions. Copy and write** *Natural materials* **or** *Manufactured materials*.

   a _____ come from nature.

   b _____ are made from natural materials which are transformed in a manufacturing process.

2 **Look at photos a–d and identify if the materials come from plants, animals or minerals. Which ones are manufactured?**

3 CD2 50 **Listen and learn about how paper is manufactured.**

4 **Match the sentences to the pictures.**

   a Next, it's mixed with special products and made into pulp.

   b After that, the pulp is dried flat.

   c Finally, the paper is made into sheets.

   d First, the wood is cut into small pieces.

Every time we make a manufactured material we're taking something from nature. If we take too many of these natural resources, they will run out. This is why it's important to use materials responsibly.

The **three Rs**: **Reduce**, **Reuse** and **Recycle** are three ways that we can be responsible consumers and look after the environment.

We should try to **reduce** the amount of materials we use and the waste we produce. Buy products with little or no packaging, then put the packaging in the correct recycling bin.

We can **reuse** many things. For example, we can reuse plastic shopping bags. We can clean packaging such as boxes and jars and use them again.

Recycle means to make something new from something we have used. If we recycle manufactured materials, it means that we can turn them into another material or product. We can recycle glass, plastic, aluminium and paper, as well as cars, electrical appliances, furniture and many more things, too.

Let's investigate! — How to recycle paper

 Investigate how we can make recycled paper.

You need:
- used paper
- water
- two containers
- a frame
- mesh
- drawing pins
- a flat, plastic sheet

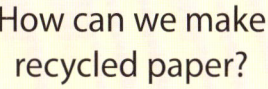
How can we make recycled paper?

a Tear the paper into small pieces and mix it with water to make a pulp.

b Collect the pulp.

c Smooth the pulp and leave it to dry.

d Carefully lift the recycled paper from the mesh.

The Science Club Recycling Centre

1 You look different today, Clara. Have you had your hair cut?

I know! You've got new glasses.

2 What are you going to do with your old glasses?

Erm … I don't know.

Did you know that you can recycle old glasses?

3 You can also recycle old mobile phones.

And computers, too. We can reuse the parts to make new computers.

Let's start the Science Club Recycling Centre!

4 The next day …

Here are my old glasses.

And here's my father with his old computer.

This is my mother's old mobile phone.

5 And here's my old mobile phone. I know how to use my new one now.

Can we think of more ways to reduce, reuse and recycle?

6 Here are some shopping bags that my mother has made! We can reduce the number of plastic bags we use.

Great!

Thank you!

There are many ways that we can help the environment by reducing, reusing and recycling the materials we use. Old glasses can be reused by people who need them, and the parts from old mobile phones can be recycled and used to make new things.

Reusing plastic bags or using fabric bags can help the environment. When we throw away plastic bags, they can harm animals that try to eat them. Can you think of other ways to reduce, reuse, recycle and help the environment?

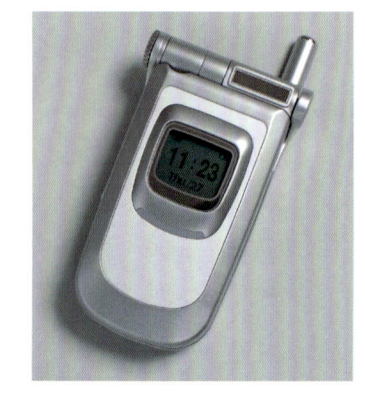

MATERIALS AROUND ME

My Science Presentation

1. **Take photos or draw pictures of materials around your home and your school.**

   a. Identify these materials and describe their properties.

   b. Are the materials natural or manufactured?

   c. What are these materials used for?

   d. ♻ How can you reduce, reuse or recycle these materials?

2. **Write a text using your information.**

3. **Use your text and photos or pictures to make a poster.**

4. **Present your poster to the class.**

MATERIALS AROUND ME

This is my ruler. I use it to draw lines. It's made of plastic. Plastic is flexible and waterproof, and it is a manufactured material. I can recycle it in the yellow recycling bin.

This is my glass. I use it to drink water. It's made of glass. Glass is fragile, transparent and waterproof, and it is a manufactured material. I can recycle it in the green recycling bin.

This is my notebook. I use it to do my homework. It's made of paper. Paper is flexible and it is a manufactured material. I can recycle it in the blue recycling bin or I can use it to make recycled paper.

Learning to learn

1 **Copy and complete the word maps.**

waterproof   manufactured   liquid   opaque   heat insulator   flexible

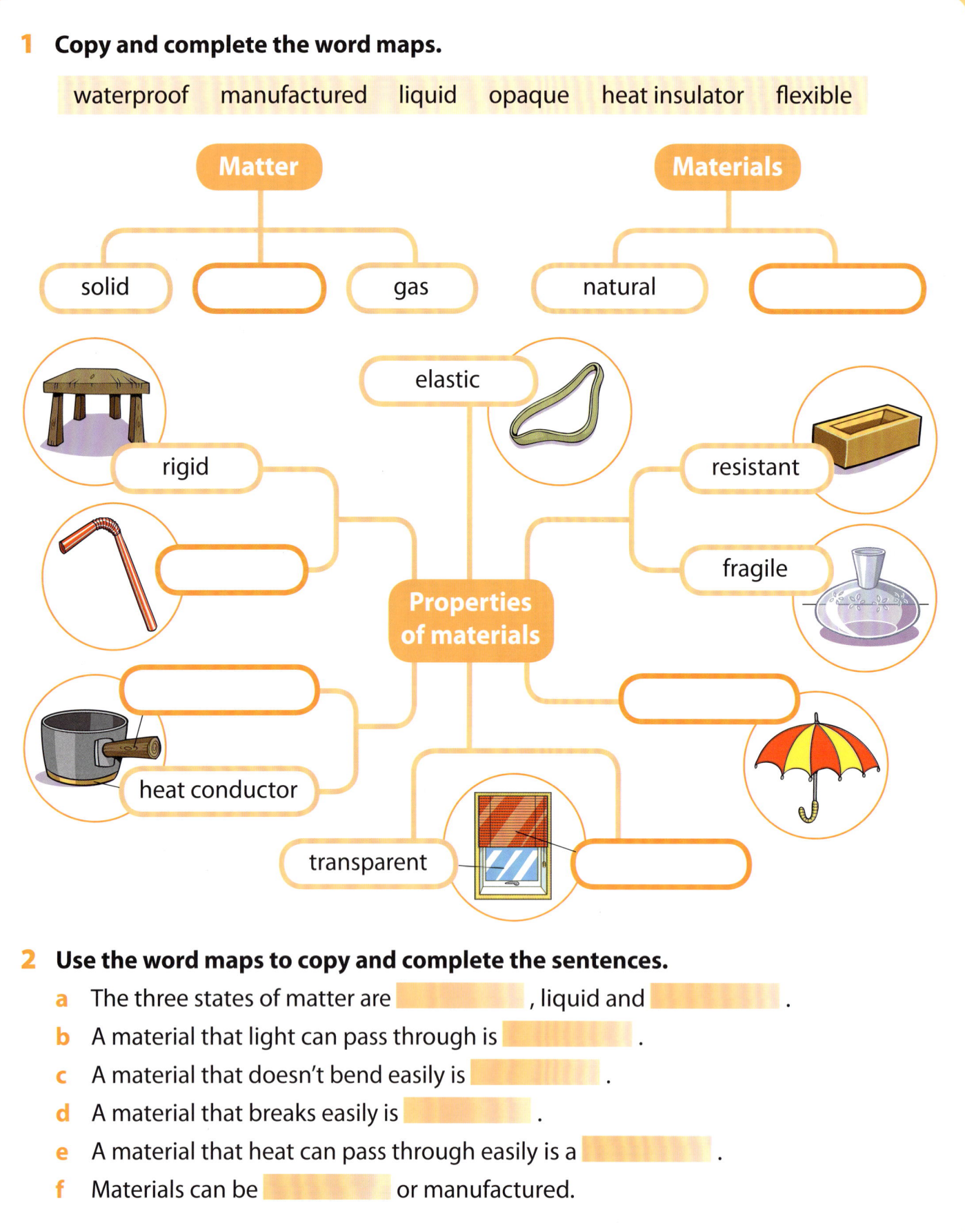

Matter
- solid
- _____
- gas

Materials
- natural
- _____

Properties of materials
- elastic
- rigid
- _____
- heat conductor
- transparent
- _____
- resistant
- fragile
- _____

2 **Use the word maps to copy and complete the sentences.**

   a The three states of matter are _____ , liquid and _____ .

   b A material that light can pass through is _____ .

   c A material that doesn't bend easily is _____ .

   d A material that breaks easily is _____ .

   e A material that heat can pass through easily is a _____ .

   f Materials can be _____ or manufactured.

3 **Copy and complete the sentences. Write *Solids*, *Liquids* or *Gases*.**

a ⬚⬚⬚⬚⬚ don't have a definite shape, but they have a definite volume.

b ⬚⬚⬚⬚⬚ have a definite shape and a definite volume.

c ⬚⬚⬚⬚⬚ don't have a definite shape and they don't have a definite volume.

4 **Copy and complete the sentences. Write *physical change* or *chemical change*.**

a A ⬚⬚⬚⬚⬚ is when matter changes shape and changes state, but the substance doesn't change.

b A ⬚⬚⬚⬚⬚ is when a new substance is produced.

5 **Look at the pictures. Are these physical changes or chemical changes? Why?**

ⓐ ⓑ

This is a ... change because ...

6 **Are these heterogeneous or homogeneous mixtures? Copy and write the correct sentences.**

ⓐ This is a **homogeneous** / **heterogeneous** mixture because **it's easy** / **it isn't possible** to see the different substances.

ⓑ This is a **homogeneous** / **heterogeneous** mixture because **it's easy** / **it isn't possible** to see the different substances.

I know the characteristics of the three states of matter. ☆ ☆ ☆

I understand how matter changes. ☆ ☆ ☆

I can identify and describe mixtures. ☆ ☆ ☆

I know some properties of materials. ☆ ☆ ☆

I'm a responsible consumer and I know the three Rs. ☆ ☆ ☆

Listen to the quiz and write the answers to the questions.

SCIENCE CLUB QUIZ

1   How many planets orbit the Sun? Can you name them all?

2   What do we call natural objects in the sky such as the Sun, planets and satellites?

3   Name two types of energy produced by the Sun.

4   What's the fastest type of energy?

5   Name three sources of renewable energy.

6   What type of machine has few or no moving parts?

7   What do we call the levers we use on a bicycle to change direction?

8   What do we call materials that heat can pass through easily?

9   What do we call materials that heat can't pass through easily?

10   What are the three Rs?

Now look at units 5, 6, 7 and 8 and check your answers.

Listen and check your answers.

How did you do?

8–10 points	5–7 points	0–4 points
Excellent	Good	Try again

SCIENCE CHALLENGE

Find a friend. Decide who is Pupil A and who is Pupil B. Take it in turns to ask and answer the questions in the Science Challenge.

PUPIL A

1 This is the third planet from the Sun.
2 These lines go horizontally around the Earth. We use these lines to measure distance from the Equator.
3 This is what happens when the moon passes between the Earth and the Sun.
4 Food contains this type of energy.
5 This type of energy will run out.
6 This machine is a circular object that turns around an axle. We use it to lift or move objects.
7 This machine is a rigid bar with a support called a fulcrum. We use it to lift or move objects.
8 This is a complex machine that allows us to make mass-produced products.
9 A new substance is produced when this type of change happens.
10 In this type of mixture it's easy to see the different substances.

PUPIL B

1 This is the Earth's satellite.
2 These lines go vertically from the North Pole to the South Pole. We use these lines to measure how far east or west a place is.
3 This is the usual weather in a place over a long period of time.
4 This type of energy travels through solid, opaque objects.
5 This type of energy will never run out.
6 This machine uses a wheel and a rope to lift or lower an object.
7 This machine is an object with at least one slanting edge. We use it to cut objects.
8 This is how much matter an object has. We can measure it in grams and in kilograms.
9 When we heat, freeze, bend, twist, stretch or squash a substance this type of change happens.
10 This type of material breaks easily.

Can you remember the definitions of these words?

efficient *(adj)* ...
expand *(verb)* ...
mass *(noun)* ...
orbit *(verb)* ...
run out *(verb)* ...
satellite *(noun)* ...
sphere *(noun)* ...
volume *(noun)* ...

Answers on Photocopiable Resources CD, Unit 8.

103

9 Living together — The school community

In this unit we're going to learn about living together and the services where we live.

In my school there are classrooms, a gym, offices, a dining room, and a playground. What's your school like?

We're all part of the **school community**. We spend a lot of our time in this community, so it's important that we all help and respect each other and make the school community a happy place where we can all learn.

In Spain, all children must go to school when they're six years old, but many children start school earlier. At school we learn a lot of things. We learn about the world around us, how to speak different languages and how to work together and respect each other. What other things do we learn at school?

The school community is made up of **pupils** and **staff**. Pupils are the children who attend school, and staff are the adults who work at the school.

Teaching staff include the **head teacher**, the **deputy head**, the **teachers** and the **secretary**. The head teacher organises the school. The deputy head helps the head teacher and also organises the teachers' classes. Different teachers teach different classes. The secretary is a teacher who works in the school office.

Non-teaching staff include the **caretaker**, the **cleaners**, the **cooks** and the **supervisors**. The caretaker and the cleaners look after the school building and the cooks prepare lunch and sometimes breakfast, too. The supervisors look after the pupils during break times.

Classroom rules

Listen to the teacher.
Do your homework.
Tidy up the classroom.

1 **What do you learn at school?**

2 **Listen to Nico at school.**

3 **Can you help Nico finish the list of classroom rules for your school?**

4 **Why do you think rules are important in the school community?**

5 **Copy and complete the sentence.**
The school community is made up of   and   .

6 **What jobs do the staff have in photos a–c?**

7 **Copy the chart and classify the people who work at a school.**

Teaching staff	Non-teaching staff

The area where we live

 We already know that we're part of the school community and that we live in villages, towns and cities. The place where we live and the villages, towns and cities around us form one area that has its own **local Government**. The head of this local Government is called the **Mayor**.

 We also have **local services**.

- **Water services** give us clean, fresh drinking water.
- **Environmental services** keep our local area clean and safe. These services include looking after sewers, street cleaning and street lighting, collecting and recycling rubbish and looking after parks and gardens.
- **Town planning services** organise and repair roads, signs, traffic lights and pavements in our local area. They also organise public transport.
- **Health services** organise hospitals and health centres.
- **Social services** help people find a home or a job. They also help elderly or disabled people who can't live alone.
- **Education services** organise schools and education centres.
- **Cultural and sports services** organise public libraries, museums and sports centres.

1  Say the *Local services* chant.

2 Look at the picture and identify the local services a–g.

3 How do you use local services?

4   Sing the *Local services* song.

In all areas of Spain, we can telephone **112** if there's an emergency like a fire, a flood or a serious accident. The person who answers the phone then sends the right emergency service to help. They can also help us over the phone until the emergency service arrives.

The **police** protect citizens. Police officers provide many services, such as fighting crime and controlling traffic. They use cars, motorbikes, horses, helicopters and boats to help them in different situations.

The **fire brigade** help when there's a fire or a flood, or when people can't get out of a vehicle or a building. The firefighters use a fire engine with fire extinguishers, ladders, pipes and cutting tools.

The **medical services** help people who suddenly need medical care, for example, in an accident. Ambulance staff travel to the sick or injured person in an ambulance that has medical equipment. They treat the patient and take them to the doctors and nurses in the hospital if necessary.

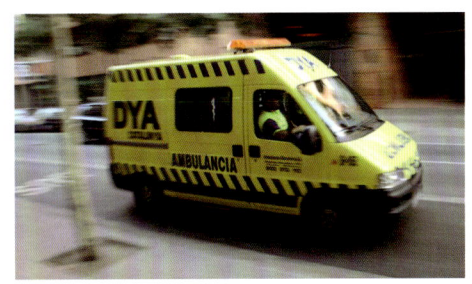

1 **Look at pictures a–e. Which emergency services can help?**

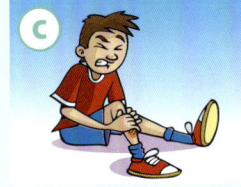

2 **Copy and complete the chart.**

	Police	Fire brigade	Medical services
What do they do?			
Who works in this service?			
What vehicle(s) do they use?			
What special equipment do they have?			

Provinces and Autonomous Communities

Which province do you live in?

What's the capital of your province?

We already know that the place where we live and the villages, towns and cities around us form one area that has its own local Government. This area and the other areas around it form a **province**. Each province has a **capital**.

N
W E
S

Guipúzcoa
A Coruña
Lugo
Asturias
Cantabria
Vizcaya
Álava
Navarra
Pontevedra
Ourense
León
Burgos
La Rioja
Huesca
Lleida
Girona
Palencia
Zamora
Soria
Zaragoza
Barcelona
Valladolid
Segovia
Tarragona
Salamanca
Guadalajara
Teruel
Ávila
Madrid
Castellón
Cáceres
Toledo
Cuenca
Valencia
Las Islas Baleares
Badajoz
Ciudad Real
Albacete
Alicante
Córdoba
Jaén
Murcia
Huelva
Sevilla
Granada
Cádiz
Málaga
Almería
Ceuta
Melilla

Las Islas Canarias
Santa Cruz de Tenerife
Las Palmas

DID YOU KNOW?

The smallest province in Spain is Guipúzcoa. Can you find this province on the map?

Which Autonomous Community do you live in?

What's the capital of your Autonomous Community?

Autonomous Communities are made up of one or more provinces. There are seventeen Autonomous Communities in Spain and two **autonomous cities**. These autonomous cities are Ceuta and Melilla. Each Autonomous Community has a **capital** and its own **Government**.

1 **How many Autonomous Communities are there in Spain?**

2 **Look at the map of Autonomous Communities. Can you find the two autonomous cities?**

3 **Can you find an Autonomous Community that is made up of just one province?**

4 **Look at the map of provinces. Which do you think is the biggest province in Spain?**

Discover

Which Autonomous Community has two capitals?
a Galicia
b Castilla-La Mancha
c Las Islas Canarias

The organisation of Autonomous Communities

Each Autonomous Community has its own **Statute of Autonomy**. The Statute of Autonomy is the most important law of an Autonomous Community. It defines the **name**, **capital**, borders and **symbols** of the Autonomous Community. The Statute of Autonomy also defines official holidays in the Autonomous Community.

> **border** *(noun)* official line that separates land.

Each Autonomous Community also has its own **Parliament**, **President** and **Government**.

The Parliament makes the laws, and the Government makes important decisions about education, health care and other services in the Autonomous Community. The Government of an Autonomous Community is made up of the President and the regional councillors.

Elections in an Autonomous Community

Citizens elect Parliament representatives.

The Parliament elects the President.

The President chooses the regional councillors.

---

1 **Which Autonomous Communities share borders with your Autonomous Community?**

2 🔍 **Find out about an official holiday in your Autonomous Community. When is it? Why is it celebrated?**

3 **Copy and complete the sentence.**
The Government of an Autonomous Community is made up of the _____ and the _____.

4 **Copy and order the sentences to describe elections in an Autonomous Community.**

a The President chooses the regional councillors.

b Citizens elect Parliament representatives.

c The Parliament elects the President.

Autonomous Communities have many things in common with each other, but there are also a lot of differences. **Festivals**, **music**, **food** and **language** can be different in different Autonomous Communities.

  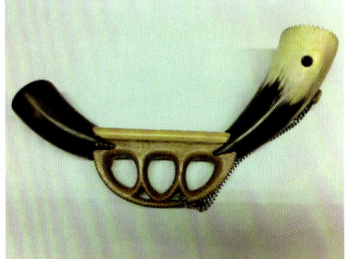 

Las Fallas is an important festival in Valencia.

The Sardana is the traditional national dance of Cataluña.

The alboka is a traditional musical instrument in Euskadi.

Cocido Madrileño is a traditional food in Madrid.

Official languages in Autonomous Communities include castellano, català, euskera and galego.

Let's investigate! — Autonomous Communities

Let's investigate how Autonomous Communities are different.

a

Buenos días.
¿Cómo estás?

b

Bos días.
Como estás?

c

Bon dia.
Com estàs?

d

Kaixo.
Egon?

a **Identify the languages in pictures a–d.**

b **Find out about your Autonomous Community.**

1   Name a traditional festival in your Autonomous Community.

2   Does your Autonomous Community have a traditional dance?

3   What traditional music does your Autonomous Community have?

4   What traditional foods does your Autonomous Community have?

5   What languages do people speak in your Autonomous Community?

6   What's the flag of your Autonomous Community like?

Which languages can you identify?

111

The forest fire

1 The Science Club is visiting a forest.

This forest is home to some protected plants and animals. Remember not to walk far.

2 I can smell the trees and the flowers, too.

I can smell smoke!

I can see smoke!

3 Look!

Quick! Let's find Professor Eco.

4 Professor Eco! Call 112! There's a fire!

5 Hello, emergency services.

I need the fire brigade. There's a fire in the forest.

6 Come on, everybody! We need to move away from the fire.

7 Well done, Science Club! You've saved the forest.

And all the plants and animals, too.

Every year **fires** destroy **forests** in Spain. These forests are important habitats for plants and animals, and the trees in the forests are important for our environment. Many fires start in the summer when forests are dry.

Don't light fires in forests. You must also never throw away glass objects. When the Sun shines on glass, it can start a fire.

MY LETTER TO THE MAYOR

1 **Think about the local services where you live.**

2 **Make a list of the services you use.**

3 **Make a list of the services you need but don't have.**

4 **Draw a chart to classify these services.**

5 **Write a letter to the Mayor.**

   a Write about which services you use.

   b Write about which services you need and say why you need these.

6 **Find photos or draw pictures to illustrate your text.**

REMEMBER!
I travel **by** bus.
I **would like to** use public transport.

	Services I use	Services I need
Water services	Drinking water	
Environmental services	Recycling near my house	Recycling near my school
Town planning services	Bus to the town centre	Bus to my school
Health services	My doctor and the hospital	
Education services	My school	
Cultural and sports services	Museum	Sports centre with swimming pool

Dear Mayor,

I live in … and I use lots of local services.

I drink clean, fresh drinking water.

I also use the recycling bins near my house to recycle rubbish.

I travel by bus to the town centre, but I would like to use public transport to go to school, too.

1 Copy and complete the word map.

head teacher   cooks   cleaners   pupils   secretary   caretaker

School community — staff

teaching staff   non-teaching staff

[ ]

deputy head   supervisor

teachers   [ ]

[ ]   [ ]

[ ]

2 Use the word map to copy and complete the sentences about the school community.

a The school community is made up of pupils and   .

b Teaching staff include the head teacher, the   , the   and the secretary.

c Non-teaching staff include the supervisor, the   , the   and the   .

3 Copy and complete the sentences about Autonomous Communities.

a Each Autonomous Community has a capital and its own   .

b The Government of an Autonomous Community is made up of the   and the   .

c Autonomous Communities are made up of one or more   .

4 Who's the head of the local Government?

5 Match and write the sentences about local services.

a	Water services	organise public libraries and sports centres.
b	Environmental services	repair streets and organise public transport.
c	Town planning services	help the elderly and the disabled.
d	Health services	organise schools and education centres.
e	Social services	organise hospitals and health centres.
f	Education services	keep our local area clean and safe.
g	Cultural and sports services	give us clean, fresh drinking water.

6 Copy and complete the sentences with the names of the emergency services.

a The _____ protect citizens.

b The _____ help when there's a fire or a flood.

c The _____ help people who suddenly need medical care.

7 Copy and complete the sentences about elections in an Autonomous Community.

a _____ elect Parliament representatives.

b The Parliament elects the _____ .

c The President chooses the _____ .

I know about the school community.   ☆ ☆ ☆

I know about local services.   ☆ ☆ ☆

I can identify different emergency services.   ☆ ☆ ☆

I can identify provinces and Autonomous Communities. ☆ ☆ ☆

I know about festivals, music, food and language in   ☆ ☆ ☆
my Autonomous Community.

In this unit we're going to learn about the Government in Spain. We're also going to learn about some important relief features of Spain.

What do you know about the Government in Spain?

We live in a **democracy**. This means that everyone has the same **rights** and **responsibilities** and people **vote** to decide things. As citizens of a democracy, we vote to decide things in the area where we live and also for the country we live in.

Citizens of a democracy have rights.

We can all vote and elect leaders.

We all have the right to have a job.

We all have access to public services, including education.

We are all protected by laws.

Citizens of a democracy have responsibilities.

tax *(noun)* money paid to the Government by citizens.

We must respect public services.

We must respect each other's cultures, religions and political beliefs.

We must pay taxes to help pay for public services.

We must respect the law.

1 What's a democracy?

2 Sing the *Democracy* song.

3 Do you think these rights and responsibilities are important? Why?

4 Can you think of any more rights and responsibilities that we have in a democracy?

Discover

How old must you be to vote in elections in Spain?
a sixteen
b eighteen
c twenty-one

The organisation of Spain

The **Constitution** was established in 1978.

The Constitution is a law and it defines:
- the rights and responsibilities of citizens
- the organisation of territories
- the organisation of the Government

As we live in a democracy, we can vote for our leaders. We can vote for:
- a Mayor in local elections
- Parliament representatives in Autonomous Community elections
- a President in general elections

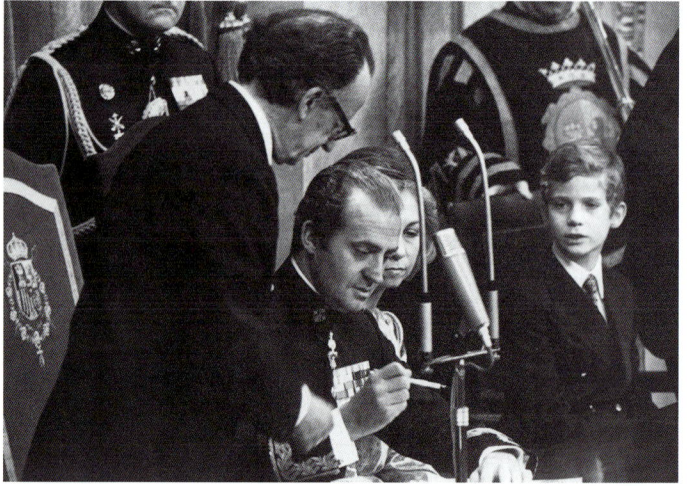

King Juan Carlos I signed the Constitution.

General elections happen every four years. Citizens vote for a   candidate   and the candidates with the most votes form a **Parliament**.

Our Parliament is called Las Cortes and is made up of a **congress** and a **senate**. The members of the congress are called **deputies**. The deputies make laws in the congress. The members of the senate are called **senators**. Senators develop the laws.

After a general election, the **President** chooses ministers to join the Government. The Government is made up of the President and the ministers.

candidate *(noun)* a person competing in an election.

---

1 **Say the *Organisation of Spain* chant.**

2 **What's the Constitution?**

3 **What does it define?**
The Constitution defines . . .

4 **Who can we vote for in a general election?**

5 **Copy and order the sentences about general elections.**

a   The President of the Government chooses ministers to join the Government.

b   The candidates with the most votes form a Parliament.

c   Citizens vote for a candidate.

🔍 **Investigate how elections work.**

How can you elect a class President?

a Work in groups to answer Nico, Clara and Yousef's questions.

b Make posters to describe and advertise your campaign.

c Elect a candidate for your group.

d Help the candidate write their speech.

e Listen to the candidates' speeches.

f Vote for a candidate.

VOTE FOR SARA!

• **RECYCLE** IN THE CLASSROOM!
• **LISTEN** TO EACH OTHER!
• **TAKE TURNS** USING THE COMPU
• **HELP** THE TEACHER TO TIDY THE CLASSROOM!

How can you make your classroom a better place?

What rights and responsibilities do you think are important?

How can you represent your class?

g Discuss the results.

1 Who's your new class President?

2 Do you think voting is a good way to elect a class President?

The geography of Spain

Spain is in the south west of Europe and its territories also include:

- two archipelagos
- two cities in the north of Africa

The **relief** of Spain's territories is very varied. There are high mountains, plains, plateaus, deserts, rivers, beaches, archipelagos and seas.

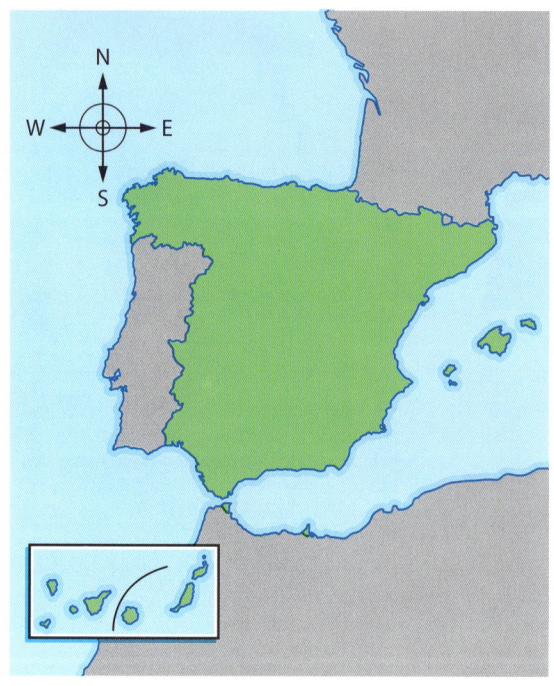

Los Pirineos are a high border between Spain and France.

La Meseta is the biggest plateau in Spain.

The only desert in Europe is in Almería in the south west of Spain.

Most beaches in Tenerife have black sand from volcanoes.

1 **Which countries does Spain share its borders with?**

2 **Can you locate and identify the two archipelagos?**

3 **Can you remember the names of the two Spanish cities in the north of Africa?**

4 **Which oceans and seas surround Spain?**

5 **What forms of relief are there where you live?**

DID YOU KNOW?

Las Islas Baleares are part of El Sistema Bético. This mountain range disappeared under the sea, and now its summits are islands!

We already know that a relief map shows the landscape in different colours to represent different forms of relief. This map uses different colours to show the   altitudes   of the forms of relief. It also shows us the main rivers.

altitude *(noun)* the height of a place or thing above sea level.

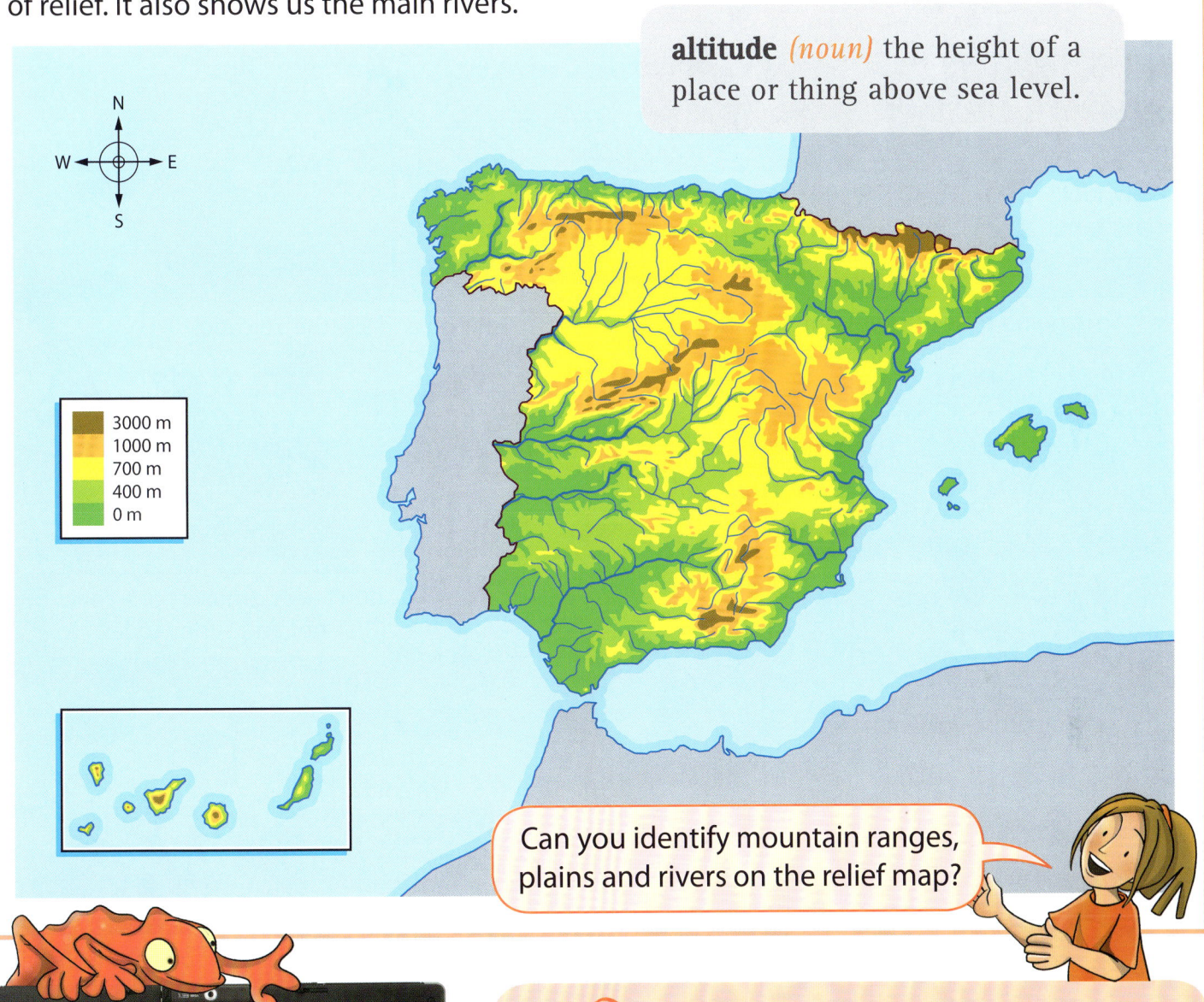

3000 m
1000 m
700 m
400 m
0 m

Can you identify mountain ranges, plains and rivers on the relief map?

Discover

Which is the longest river in Spain?
a El Guadalquivir
b El Ebro
c El Duero

1   **Look at the relief map. Name the highest mountain ranges.**

2   **Copy the chart and classify the rivers.**
a Which rivers flow into the Atlantic Ocean?
b Which rivers flow into the Mediterranean Sea?

Flow into the Atlantic Ocean	Flow into the Mediterranean Sea

The volcano

1 The Science Club is on a trip in Tenerife.

Wow, look! Black sand!

That's because the sand comes from a volcano on the island.

2 Volcano?

Where?

3 We're going to see the volcano this afternoon.

Great!

4 Let's go and see the volcano.

I don't need trousers or a coat. It's hot and sunny today.

5 Look! The volcano!

6 I'm cold.

Look at the view!

Look at Nico!

El Teide is in Tenerife and it's the highest volcano in Spanish territory. It's also the third-biggest volcano in the world! El Teide last erupted in 1909.

The volcano and the area around it is now a National Park. Although Tenerife has a sub-tropical climate, it can be very cold when you go up El Teide!

MY AUTONOMOUS COMMUNITY

1  **Write a text about your Autonomous Community.**

  a What's the capital of your Autonomous Community?

  b Describe and draw its flag.

  c Describe festivals, music, languages and food in your Autonomous Community.

  d Describe the relief in your Autonomous Community and name some of these forms of relief.

2 **Find photos or draw pictures to illustrate your text.**

REMEMBER!

The capital of . . .
is . . .

Relief and rivers

Capital

My Autonomous Community

Languages

Food

Festivals

Flag

Music

123

1 **Copy and complete the word map.**

vote   congress   ministers   senators   rights

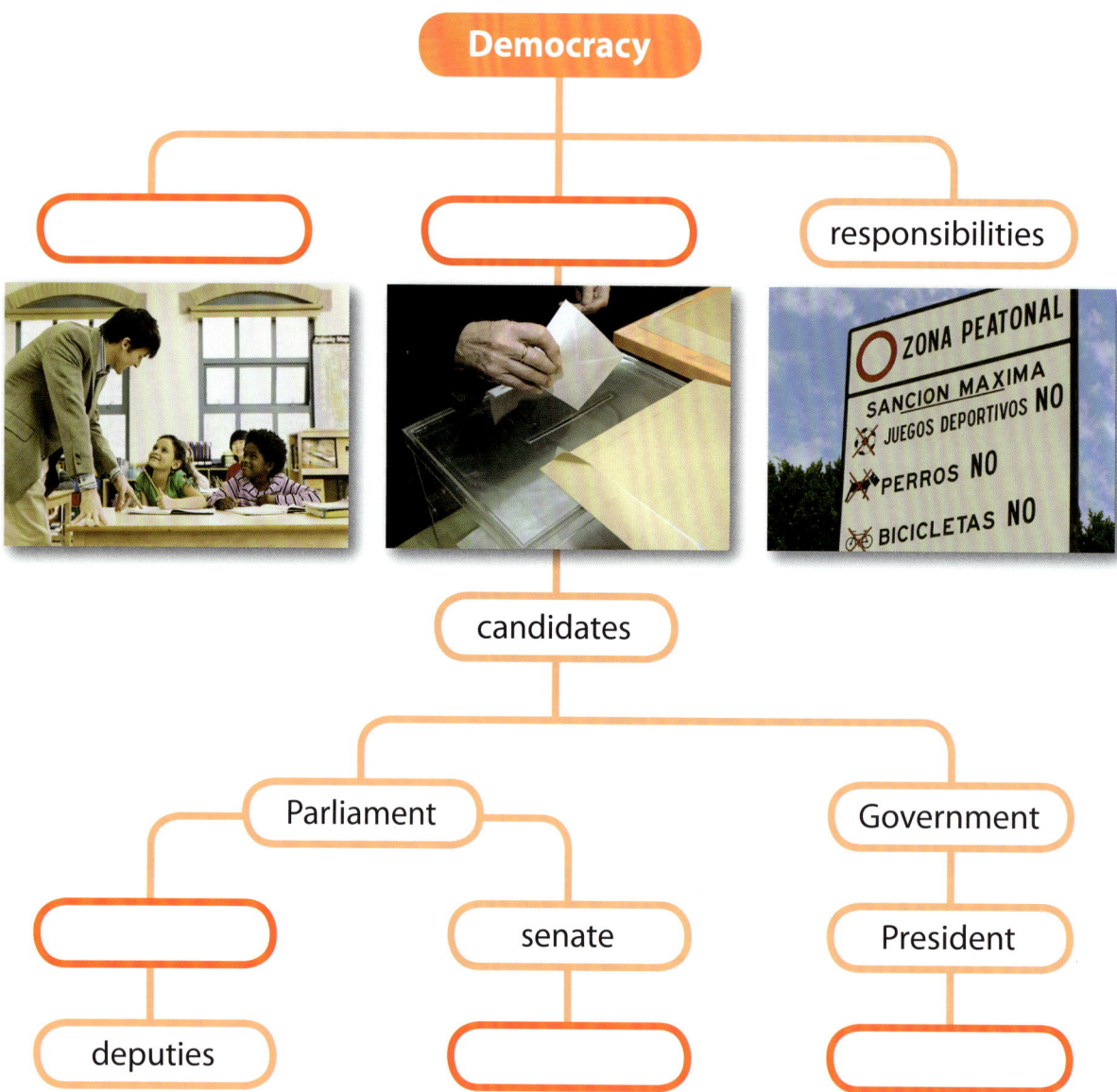

Democracy

responsibilities

candidates

Parliament

Government

senate

President

deputies

2 **Use the word map to copy and complete the sentences.**

a The _____ with the most votes form a _____ .

b Our Parliament is called Las Cortes and is made up of a _____ and a senate.

c The members of the congress are called _____ .

d The members of the _____ are called senators.

e The Government is made up of the _____ and the _____ .

3 **Copy the chart and classify the rights and responsibilities of citizens in a democracy.**

Rights	Responsibilities

- Have the right to have a job.
- Pay taxes to help pay for public services.
- Respect other people's cultures, religions and political beliefs.
- Have access to public services, including education.
- Vote and elect leaders.
- Respect the law.
- Respect public services.
- Be protected by laws.

4 **Copy and complete the sentences about who we can vote for in a democracy.**

Mayor   President   Parliament representatives

a We can vote for a .... in local elections.
b We can vote for .... in Autonomous Community elections.
c We can vote for a .... in general elections.

5 **Which is the odd one out? Why?**
a **El Mar Cantábrico / El Mar Mediterráneo / El Sistema Bético**
b **La Cordillera Costero-Catalana / El Guadalquivir / Los Pirineos**
c **El Duero / El Ebro / El Océano Atlántico**

... is the odd one out because ...

I know about rights and responsibilities in a democracy.   ☆ ☆ ☆

I know about the organisation of Spain.   ☆ ☆ ☆

I know about the geography of Spanish territories.   ☆ ☆ ☆

I can identify some forms of relief in Spanish territories.   ☆ ☆ ☆

In this unit we're going to learn about population and how and why it changes.

The **population** of a place is how many **inhabitants** there are in that area. The inhabitants of a place are all the people who live there; children, adults and elderly people.

Different places have different populations. Populations can be big or small. We can talk about the populations of the villages, towns and cities where we live, our local areas, our provinces, our Autonomous Communities, our country, and even the population of the whole world!

The population of a place is made up of people of different ages. We can classify these people in three ways:

The **child population** is made up of children and adolescents under sixteen years old.

The **adult population** is made up of people over sixteen years old and people under sixty-five years old.

The **elderly population** is made up of people over sixty-five years old.

What can you see in the photos?

a

b

Another way to classify population is into the **urban population** and the **rural population**. Most of Spain's population is urban, which means that most people live in towns and cities. These people usually work in the secondary and tertiary sectors. They work in industry or provide a service.

The rural population is made up of the people who live in villages. These people usually work in the primary sector. They work in agriculture, livestock farming or fishing.

1 **What does population mean?**
The population of a place is …

2 **Are you part of the child, adult or elderly population?**
I'm part of the … because …

3 **Look at photos a and b and listen to Clara and Nico. Which photos are they talking about?**

4 **Are you part of the rural population or the urban population?**

5 **Are you part of the active population or the inactive population?**

6 **Say the *Population* chant.**

We can also classify population into the **active population** and the **inactive population**. The active population is made up of the people who work and receive a salary, and the people who are unemployed and looking for work. The inactive population is made up of the people who can't work, such as children and the elderly, and the people who do voluntary work.

unemployed *(adj)* without a job.

Population changes

The population of a place can increase or decrease .

If the number of babies born is bigger than the number of people that die, the population increases.

If the number of babies born is smaller than the number of people that die, the population decreases.

increase *(verb)* to get bigger in amount or number.

decrease *(verb)* to get smaller in amount or number.

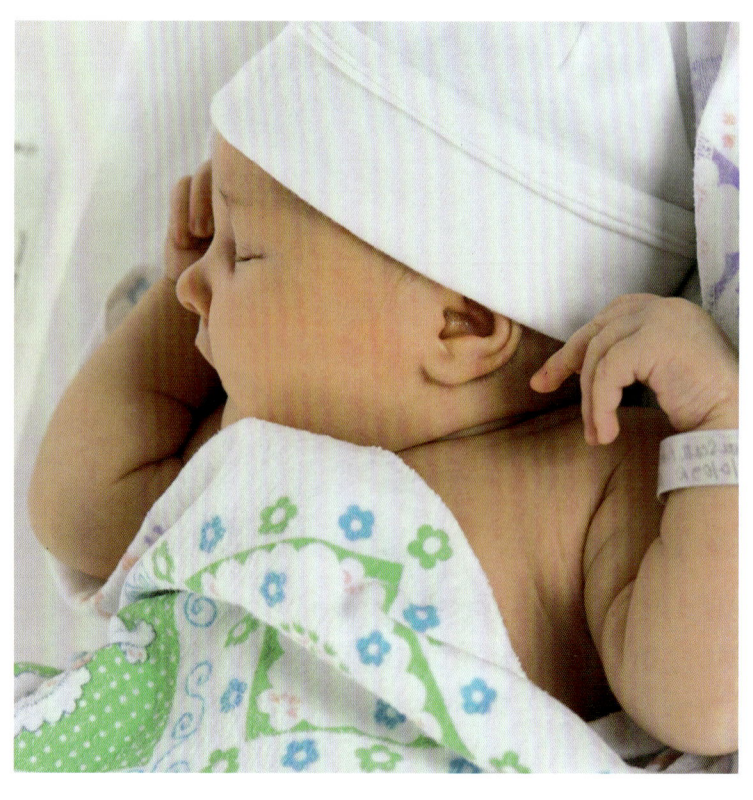

Discover

What's the population of Spain?

a more than 25 million
b more than 35 million
c more than 45 million

DID YOU KNOW?

The elderly population of Spain is increasing and the child population of Spain is decreasing.

We already know that many people move from villages to towns and cities for work. Some people even move to a different country! People who leave our country to live in a new place are called **emigrants**. People who move from their country to live in our country are called **immigrants**.

1. My father is an immigrant to Spain. He lived in a small town in a different country.

2. There were few jobs in this town, so my father came to Spain.

3. At first it was difficult, but my father learnt Spanish.

HOLA ,BUENOS DÍAS.

4. He found a job.

5. He found a house, made new friends, married my mother and had a family!

6. Now my father is very happy and we visit my grandparents every year!

1 Copy and complete the sentences.

a If the number of babies born is bigger than the number of people that die, the population ▨▨▨▨ .

b If the number of babies born is smaller than the number of people that die, the population ▨▨▨▨ .

2 Why do you think people emigrate?

3 Listen to Yousef talking about his father.

4 Why do you think life can be difficult for immigrants?

5 Does the population increase or decrease? Copy the words and write ↑ for increase and ↓ for decrease.

a People die.

b Immigrants arrive.

c Babies are born.

d Emigrants leave.

6 Say the *Population* rap.

A growing population

The human population is growing. A growing population needs more houses and more space for people to live in, more food and more natural resources from the Earth.

We need to protect the natural landscapes on Earth. It's our responsibility to look after our planet.

- Respect plants and animals and protected areas.
- Use natural sources of energy.
- Use public transport.
- Remember the 3 Rs! Reduce, Reuse, Recycle!

1 **What does a growing population need?**
  A growing population needs . . .

2 **Look at the picture and identify how people have changed the landscape.**

3 **How can a growing population damage the Earth?**

4 **How can we look after our planet?**

A **census** can tell us the number of inhabitants in a province, in an Autonomous Community or in the whole country. A census is a survey of all the inhabitants of a place and there's a census every ten years. A census is important because it includes everyone at the same time and asks everyone the same questions. This makes it easy to compare different parts of the country. The information from a census helps Governments plan services for the inhabitants.

Investigate the population of your household.

a Find out how many people in your household are:

1 under sixteen years old.

2 between sixteen years old and sixty-five years old.

3 over sixty-five years old.

b Collect the information from everyone in your class.

c Draw a bar chart with the information for your whole class.

d Discuss the results:

1 Which group is the biggest / smallest?

2 Why do you think this is?

> How can you classify the population of your household?

A new pupil

1 This is Alisa. She's from Germany and today is her first day at our school.

Population

2 Hello. I'm Clara.

Hello.

3 Alisa! Do you want to play with us?

Yes, please.

This is Nico and this is Yousef.

Hello.

4 It's very hot.

Hot? Today isn't hot! It's warm!

The weather in my country is very different!

5 What's this?

It's tortilla. Try it.

It's delicious! The food in my country is very different.

6 Goodbye. See you at school tomorrow.

But tomorrow's Saturday. There's no school.

In my country I go to school on Saturday. I think I'm going to like my new school!

Today, many people emigrate for work. Immigrants often have to learn a new language, find a new home and make new friends. They also have to learn about different customs and different foods.

Life in a new country can be interesting, but it can also be hard. How can we make people feel welcome in our country?

132

CREATE A CLASS CENSUS

Remember that a census is important because it includes everyone at the same time and asks everyone the same questions.

Information from a class census can help you and your teacher plan events and activities for your class. A class census can also help plan for the needs of everyone in the classroom.

1 **Use these notes to make a list of questions for the census.**

2 **Add some other questions that you think are important.**

3 **Use these questions to create one census for your class.**

4 **Complete the census.**

5  **Write a text to summarise the information in your completed census.**

Name

Male or female

Age and date of birth

Favourite Science topic

I need help with this Science topic

Favourite Science activity

My name is Alba González Montero. I'm ten years old and my date of birth is 30th March . . .

My favourite Science topic is matter, but I need help with plants and photosynthesis.

My favourite activity in Science is Let's investigate! I also like Learning to learn activities.

REMEMBER!

I'm ten years old.
My **date of birth is** . . .

1 **Copy and complete the word map.**   urban   elderly   active   adult   rural

inactive

Population

child

2 **Use the word map to copy and complete the sentences.**

a The _____ is made up of adolescents and children under sixteen years old.

b The _____ is made up of people over sixteen years old and people under sixty-five years old.

c The _____ is made up of people over sixty-five years old.

d The _____ is made up of people who live in towns and cities.

e The _____ is made up of people who live in villages.

f The _____ is made up of people who work and receive a salary, and people who are unemployed and looking for work.

g The _____ is made up of people who can't work, such as children and the elderly, and people who do voluntary work.

3 **Copy and complete the sentences.**

   a The ▓▓▓▓▓ of a place is how many inhabitants there are in that area.

   b The ▓▓▓▓▓ of a place are all the people who live there: children, adults and elderly people.

4 **Copy and complete the information about a census.**

A census is a survey of all the ▓▓▓▓▓ of a place and there's a census every ▓▓▓▓▓ years. A census is important because it includes everyone at the same time and asks everyone the same questions. This makes it easy to compare different parts of the country. The information from a census helps Governments plan ▓▓▓▓▓ for the inhabitants.

5 **How does population increase and decrease? Copy and complete the chart.**

Babies are born   People die   Emigration   Immigration

Population increases	Population decreases

6 **Name three things that a growing population needs.**

A growing population needs . . .

7 **Name three things we can do to look after our planet.**

To look after our planet we can . . .

I know how to classify population. ☆ ☆ ☆

I understand how populations change. ☆ ☆ ☆

I know how a growing population can affect the Earth and its natural resources. ★ ★ ☆

I know why a census is important. ☆ ☆ ☆

In this unit we're going to learn about history. We're going to learn about how people lived in the past, and about some important events and people in history.

History is everything that happened in the past. History is important because we can learn from the past. We can understand why things happen in our world and use this information to make our lives better.

We can use **historical sources** to learn about history. Historical sources are objects that give us information about the past. Historical sources can be photos, paintings, written documents, buildings or objects that people used in the past.

We can use **measurements of time** to organise information about the past.

- A **year** is made up of **twelve months**.
- A **decade** is made up of **ten years**.
- A **century** is made up of **one hundred years**.
- A **millennium** is made up of **one thousand years**.

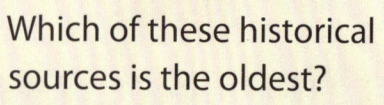

Which of these historical sources is the oldest?

We can divide history into five main periods: **Prehistory**, **Ancient history**, the **Middle Ages**, the **Modern Age** and the **Contemporary Age**.

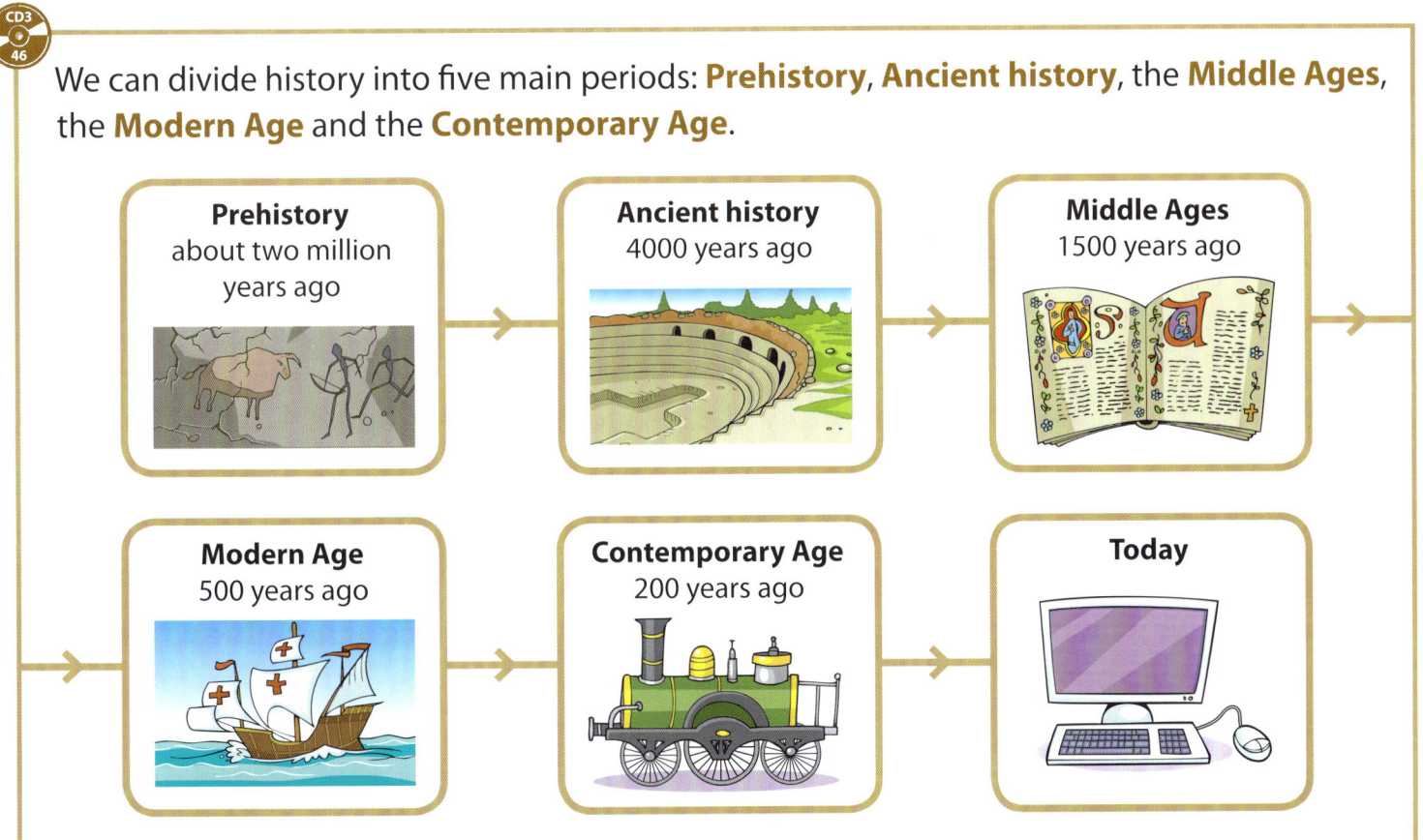

Prehistory
about two million years ago

Ancient history
4000 years ago

Middle Ages
1500 years ago

Modern Age
500 years ago

Contemporary Age
200 years ago

Today

---

1   **What is history?**

2   **Why is history important?**

History is important because . . .

3   **Look at photos a–e. Order the historical sources from the oldest to the most recent.**

4   **Match and write the sentences.**

a	A year	ten years.
b	A decade	one thousand years.
c	A century	is made up of	twelve months.
d	A millennium	one hundred years.

5   Say the *Periods of history* chant.

6   **Order the five main periods of history from the earliest to the most recent.**
Middle Ages / Contemporary Age / Prehistory / Modern Age / Ancient history

7   **Which period do you think we know the least about? Why?**

8   **Can you match the historical sources in photos a–e to the periods of history?**

Prehistory

We already know what history is, but what is **prehistory**? Prehistory is the period from when the first humans existed about two million years ago, until the invention of writing.

Although people living during this period couldn't write, they could leave some historical sources. These historical sources mean that we can learn about prehistory.

There were two main periods of prehistory: the **Palaeolithic period** and the **Neolithic period**.

In the Palaeolithic period, people were **nomads**. This means that they moved from place to place to look for food and shelter. They used stone, wood and bones to make **simple tools**.

In the Neolithic period, people started to live in one place and **form communities**. They started to grow **crops** and keep **domestic animals**. They used stone and metal to make more **complex tools**.

Palaeolithic period

Neolithic period

1 **What is prehistory?**

2 **What are the two main periods of prehistory?**

   The two main periods of prehistory are . . .

3 **Look at the pictures of the Palaeolithic period and the Neolithic period. Copy the chart and classify the differences between them.**

Palaeolithic period	Neolithic period

Ancient history began more than four thousand years ago, when people invented **writing**. During this time, the first civilisations developed in countries such as Greece, Egypt, China and Mexico.

People in these first civilisations lived together in communities and didn't have to move from place to place to find food and shelter. This meant that they had time to build **cities** with public and private buildings, write **laws**, develop **skills** and have **jobs**.

Egyptian hieroglyphs

civilisation *(noun)* a society that shares the same culture and institutions.

One of the most important civilisations in ancient history was the **Roman civilisation**. Roman territory was called the **Roman Empire** and the capital of the Roman Empire was **Rome**. The Romans had a strong army and this helped increase their territory. The Romans arrived in the Iberian Peninsula about two thousand years ago.

a The Romans built outdoor theatres called **amphitheatres** where people watched fights between gladiators, and between gladiators and wild animals.

b The Romans built **stone roads** to connect cities.

c The Romans built **bridges** over rivers.

d The Romans built **aqueducts** to carry water from rivers and lakes to cities.

DID YOU KNOW?

The Romans brought their language, Latin, to the Iberian Peninsula. In Science, many plants and animals have Latin names.

"MY SCIENTIFIC NAME IS PROBOSCIDEA ELEPHANTIDAE!"

1 Why do you think the invention of writing was important?

2 Name three things that people in the first civilisations did.

People in the first civilisations . . .

3 Look at pictures a–d. How are these constructions different from the ones we use today?

The Middle Ages

The **Middle Ages** began about 1500 years ago. During this period, two civilisations lived in the Iberian Peninsula: the **Christian civilisation** and the **Islamic civilisation**.

The Christian civilisation in the Iberian Peninsula began when the Romans arrived. Christian Spain was divided into areas called **kingdoms**. Each of these kingdoms had a **king**. The kingdoms attacked each other, so people built castles and walls to defend their towns and cities.

The Christian civilisation built religious buildings such as **churches** and **cathedrals**.

During this period, there were four groups of Christians:

a The **nobles** owned land given to them by the king. They lived in castles.

b The **clergy** were the religious people of the Middle Ages. They looked after their own land and helped the poor. They could often read and write in Latin.

c The **craftsmen** were skilled workers and made products from materials such as glass and wood. The **merchants** traded products such as metal and textiles.

d The **peasants** worked hard on the land of the nobles. The peasants didn't receive a salary, but the nobles gave them protection.

The Islamic civilisation in the Iberian Peninsula began when the Muslims arrived from the north of Africa. The Islamic civilisation built religious buildings such as **mosques**.

---

1 **What were the four groups of Christians in the Middle Ages?**

The four groups of Christians in the Middle Ages were . . .

2 Look at pictures a–d. **Which people do you think were the richest? Why?**

3 Look at pictures a–d. **Which people do you think were the poorest? Why?**

4 **What religious buildings did the Christian and Islamic civilisations build?**

The **Modern Age** began about five hundred years ago. Small kingdoms came together to form big **countries** with one king, and these countries started to explore the world. This period was a time of **discovery** and **scientific invention**.

Inventions such as the **compass** and more **accurate maps** meant that people could travel to new places without getting lost, and discover new lands and new products.

In 1492, an **explorer** called Christopher Columbus sailed west in his ship. He wanted to travel around the world to reach Asia in the east, but instead Columbus travelled west and reached the New World which we now call America.

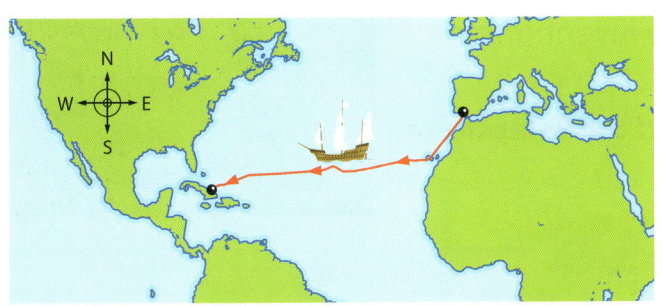

An important invention of the Modern Age was **Gutenberg's printing press**. This invention meant that it was quicker and cheaper to produce books and maps.

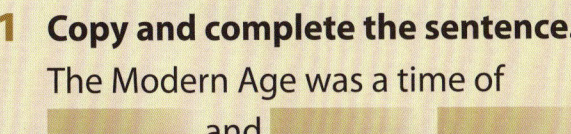

1 **Copy and complete the sentence.**
The Modern Age was a time of _____ and _____ .

2 **Why were the compass and accurate maps important to the Modern Age?**

3 **Where did Columbus want to travel?**

4 **Why did more people learn to read in the Modern Age?**

Discover
Which two products didn't Spain have before the Modern Age?
a potatoes and tomatoes
b rice and oranges
c wheat and grapes

The Contemporary Age

The **Contemporary Age** began about two hundred years ago and was a time of **industry** and **changes in society**. New inventions like the steam engine changed the way that people lived and worked.

The steam engine made work quicker and easier. It was used in machines and transport.

Factories made mass-produced products. People moved to towns and cities for work and urban populations increased.

Cities grew and changed. There were new streets and shops. There were services such as schools, hospitals and public transport.

There were also important scientific inventions during this period, such as the discovery of electricity. Some inventions in medicine included the **x-ray** and vaccinations . Some inventions in communication were the **radio** and the **telephone**.

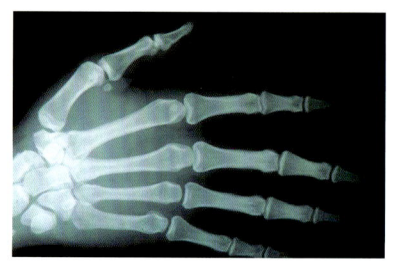

vaccination *(noun)* protection against a disease.

1 What advantages and disadvantages did industry bring to people's lives?

2 Copy the chart and classify these inventions of the Contemporary Age.

vaccinations   radio   telephone   x-ray

Inventions in medicine	Inventions in communication

3 Can you imagine life before electricity?

4 Sing the *Periods of history* song.

Investigate people in history.

Do you know about these important people in history?

Diego Rodríguez de Silva y Velázquez

Hernán Cortés de Monroy y Pizarro

Miguel de Cervantes Saavedra

Miguel Servet

a Look at the pictures.

1 What period of history did these people live in?
2 What did they do?
3 Why were they important?

Scientist?

Artist?

Explorer?

Writer?

b Discuss the results. Copy and complete the chart.

Name	Period of history	Profession	Important because …

Treasure!

1 The Science Club is visiting some Roman ruins.

Who's that, Professor Eco?

That's the Emperor. The Emperor was the head of the Roman Empire.

2

What's that, Professor Eco?

That's a Roman temple. This is where the Romans worshipped their gods.

3 What's that, Professor Eco?

That's a Roman floor. This is part of a house where Romans lived.

4 What's that, Professor Eco?

That's a Roman amphitheatre. That's where the Romans watched gladiators and wild animals fight.

5 What's that, Professor Eco?

That's Roman money! We must give it to the museum.

6 A few days later …

Roman treasure discovered by Science Club!

Although the Roman Empire ended over 1500 years ago, we can still see the remains of Roman buildings.

The amphitheatre was the centre of entertainment in Roman times. People went to the amphitheatre to watch fights between gladiators and wild animals. Gladiators were people trained to fight other gladiators or wild animals, such as lions and bears.

A BUILDING FROM THE PAST

1 **Make a poster about an old building near where you live.**

2 **Write a text describing the building.**
   a Which period was it built in?
   b What was it used for?
   c What is it used for now?
   d How has this building changed?

3 **Take photos or draw pictures to illustrate your text.**

4 **Present your poster to the class.**

My Science Presentation

THE AQUEDUCT IN SEGOVIA

This is a building from ancient times. It is an aqueduct and was built by the Romans.

It is very high and it is made of stone. It carried water from the Río Frío over 10 km to Segovia.

The aqueduct was used until very recently but now lots of tourists visit it and take photos.

Learning to learn

1 **Copy and complete the word map.**

> Neolithic period   Christian civilisation   Palaeolithic period   Islamic civilisation
> peasants   industry   clergy   Roman civilisation   scientific invention

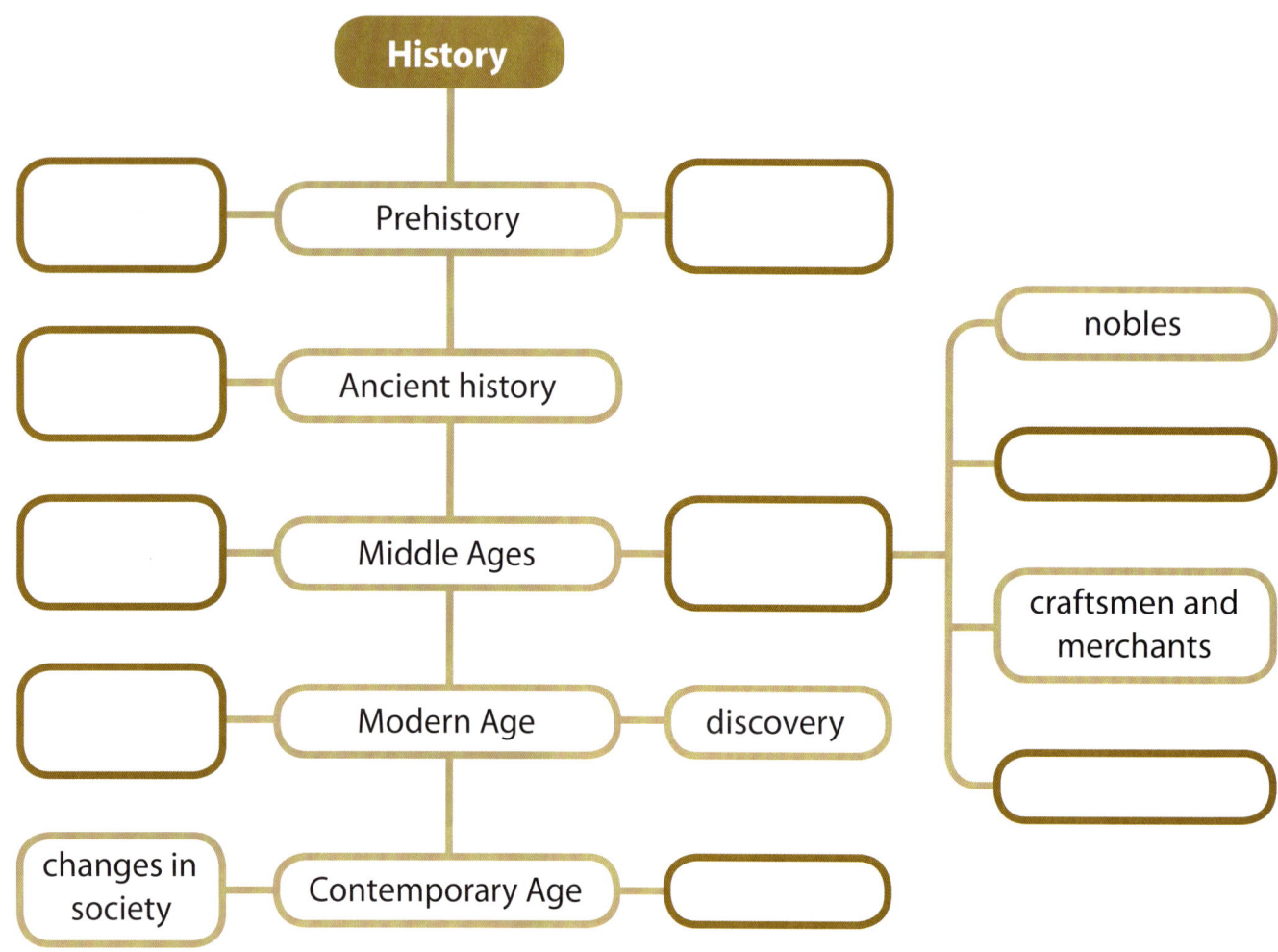

History

Prehistory

Ancient history

Middle Ages

Modern Age — discovery

changes in society — Contemporary Age

nobles

craftsmen and merchants

2 **Use the word map to copy and complete the sentences.**

a The two main periods of prehistory are the ▨▨▨▨▨ period and the ▨▨▨▨▨ period.

b One of the most important civilisations in Ancient history was the ▨▨▨▨▨ civilisation.

c The two civilisations in the Iberian Peninsula during the Middle Ages were the ▨▨▨▨▨ civilisation and the ▨▨▨▨▨ civilisation.

d The Modern Age was a time of ▨▨▨▨▨ and scientific ▨▨▨▨▨.

e The Contemporary Age was a time of ▨▨▨▨▨ and ▨▨▨▨▨.

3 **Copy and classify the sentences about the periods of prehistory.**

a People started to grow crops and keep domestic animals.

b People were nomads.

c They made more complex tools.

d They made simple tools.

e People formed communities.

Palaeolithic period	Neolithic period

4 **Copy and complete the sentences about the Roman civilisation.**

aqueducts   bridges   roads   amphitheatres

a The Romans built outdoor theatres called ▮▮▮▮ .

b The Romans built stone ▮▮▮▮ to connect cities.

c The Romans built ▮▮▮▮ over rivers.

d The Romans built ▮▮▮▮ to carry water from rivers and lakes to cities.

5 **Copy and complete the sentences about the Middle Ages.**

The Christian civilisation in the Iberian Peninsula began when the ▮▮▮▮ arrived. The Islamic civilisation in the Iberian Peninsula began when the ▮▮▮▮ arrived.

6 **What invention of the Modern Age meant that it was quicker and cheaper to produce books and maps?**

7 **Write four important scientific inventions of the Contemporary Age.**

Four important scientific inventions of the Contemporary Age were . . .

I know what history is and understand why it's important.

I can use measurements of time to organise information about the past.

I can identify the five main periods of history.

I know about some important events and people in history.

Listen to the quiz and write the answers to the questions.

SCIENCE CLUB QUIZ

1 Who is the head of the local Government?

2 What are Autonomous Communities made up of?

3 What's the most important law of an Autonomous Community?

4 What law was established in 1978?

5 How often do general elections happen?

6 What do we call a survey of all the inhabitants in a place?

7 How do we classify the people who work and receive a salary?

8 Name three different historical sources that give us information about the past.

9 What were the two main periods of prehistory?

10 What were the four groups of Christians in the Middle Ages?

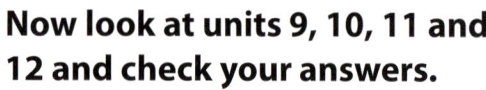

Now look at units 9, 10, 11 and 12 and check your answers.

Listen and check your answers.

How did you do?

8–10 points	5–7 points	0–4 points
Excellent	Good	Try again

SCIENCE CHALLENGE

Find a friend. Decide who is Pupil A and who is Pupil B. Take it in turns to ask and answer the questions in the Science Challenge.

PUPIL A

1. These local services give us clean, fresh drinking water.
2. These local services help people find a home or a job.
3. This emergency service protects citizens from crime.
4. In a general election the candidates with the most votes form this.
5. These people are the members of the senate.
6. This population is made up of adolescents and children under sixteen years old.
7. This population is made up of people over sixty-five years old.
8. This population is made up of the people who live in towns and cities.
9. This period began when people invented writing.
10. This period was a time of discovery and scientific invention.

PUPIL B

1. These local services organise hospitals and health centres.
2. These local services organise schools and education centres.
3. In a democracy we do this to decide things.
4. These people are the members of the congress.
5. This is made up of the President and the ministers.
6. This population is made up of people over sixteen years old and people under sixty-five years old.
7. This population is made up of the people who live in villages.
8. This period is from when the first humans existed until the invention of writing.
9. During this period, the Christian and Islamic civilisations lived in the Iberian Peninsula.
10. This period was a time of industry and changes in society.

Can you remember the definitions of these words?

altitude *(noun)* ...
border *(noun)* ...
candidate *(noun)* ...
civilisation *(noun)* ...
decrease *(verb)* ...
increase *(verb)* ...
tax *(noun)* ...
unemployed *(adj)* ...
vaccination *(noun)* ...

Answers on Photocopiable Resources CD, Unit 12.

Food groups

bread and cereals

fruit and vegetables

meat and fish

milk and dairy

sugary foods

Nutrients

Calcium is an important mineral for healthy bones and teeth.

Carbohydrates give us energy.

Fats give us energy.

Proteins are for our growth.

Vitamins and minerals are for our health.

The digestive system

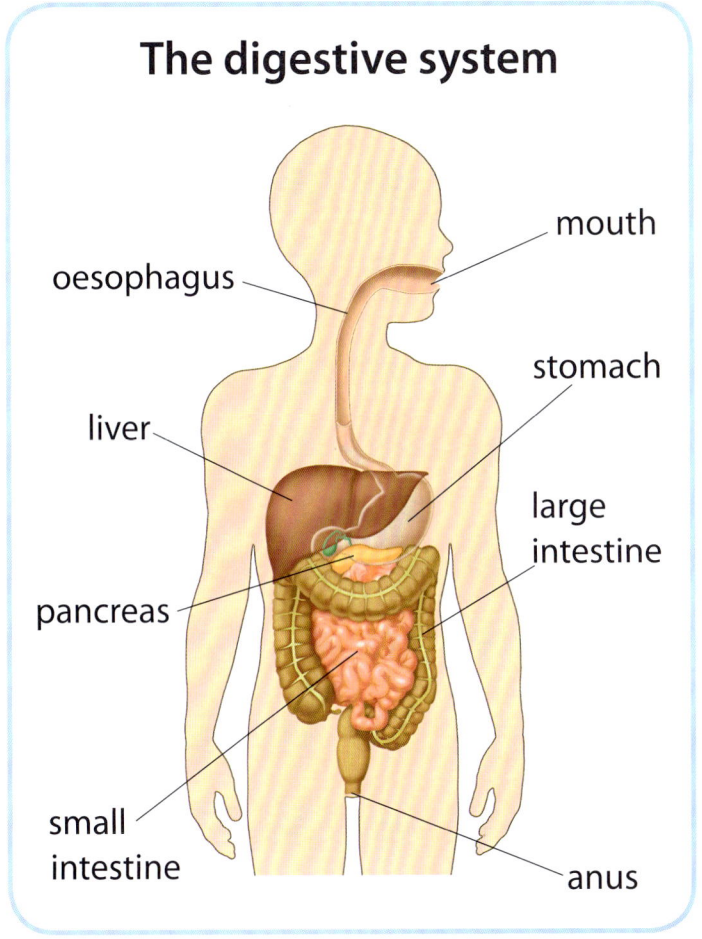

- mouth
- oesophagus
- stomach
- liver
- large intestine
- pancreas
- small intestine
- anus

The excretory system

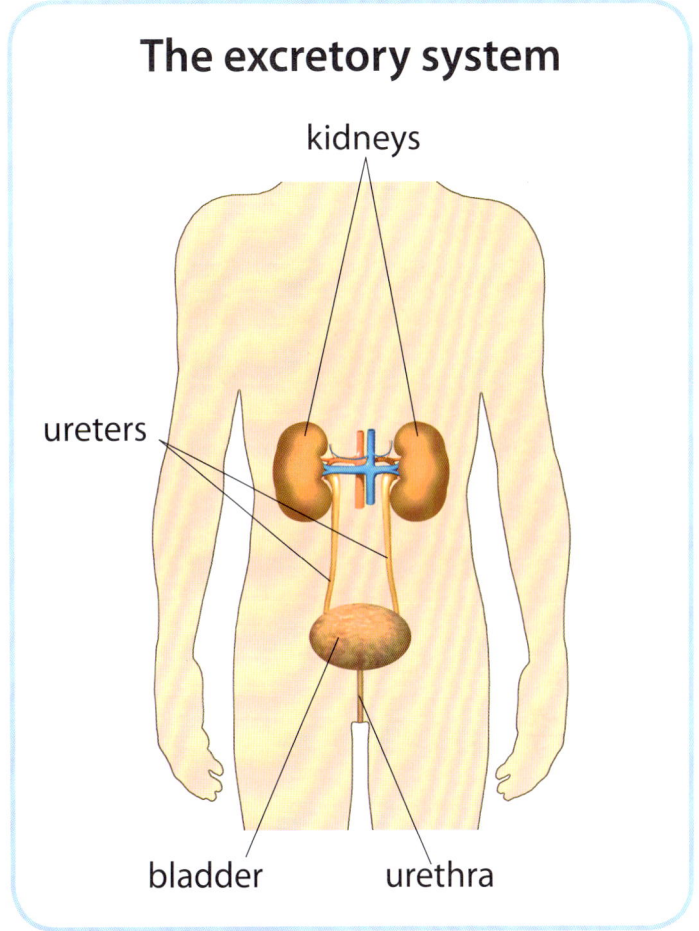

- kidneys
- ureters
- bladder
- urethra

Milk teeth

- incisors
- canines
- canines
- molars
- incisors

Permanent teeth

- incisors
- canines
- premolars
- molars
- premolars
- canines
- incisors

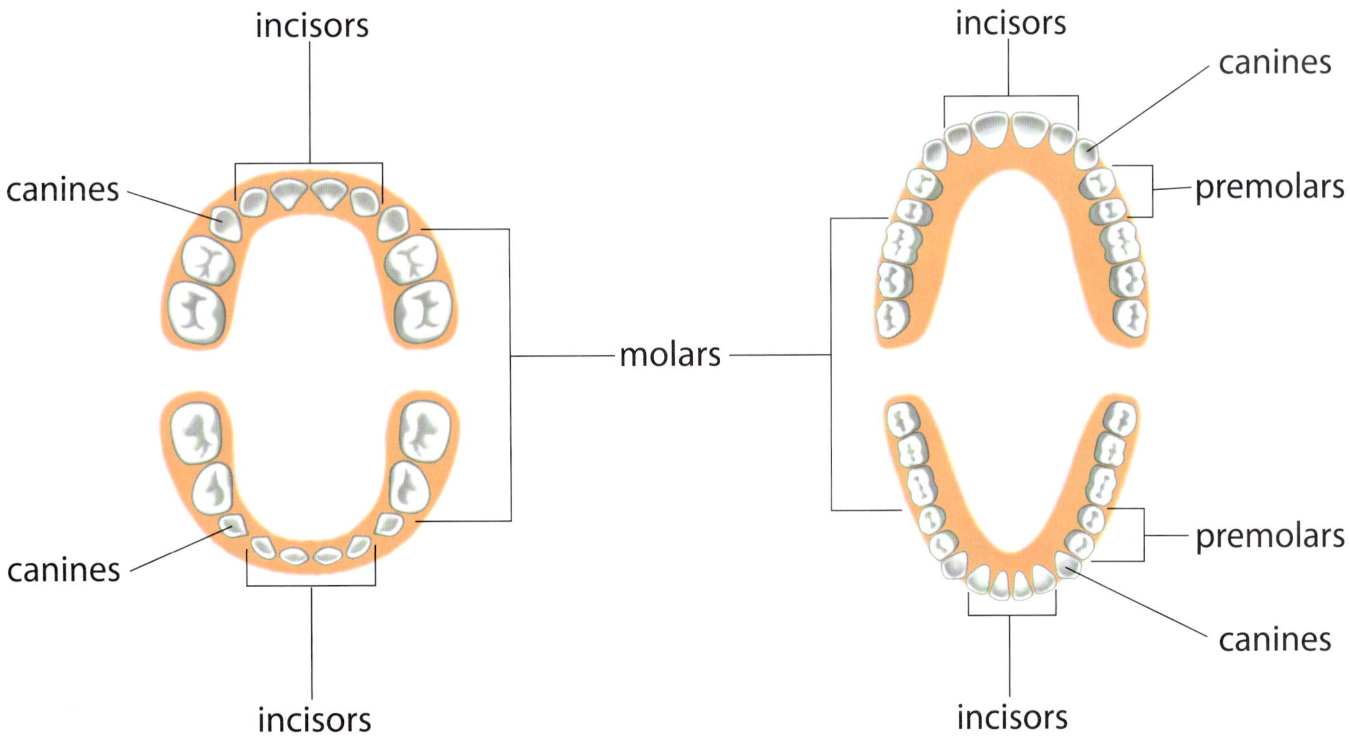

The stages of life.

babies

children

adolescents

adults

elderly people

The circulatory system and the heart

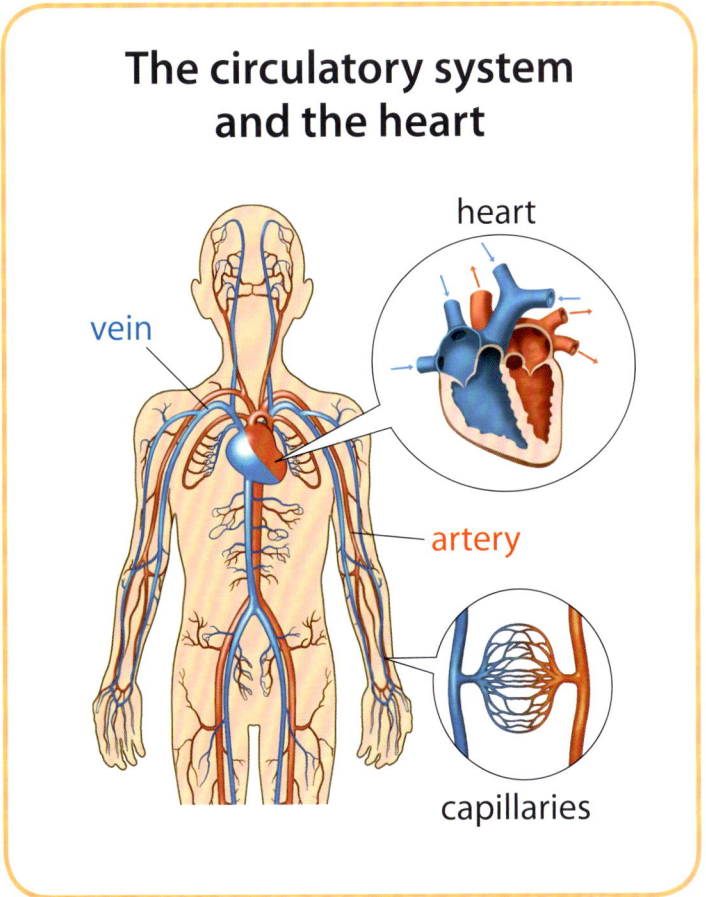

vein

heart

artery

capillaries

The reproductive systems

The male reproductive organs

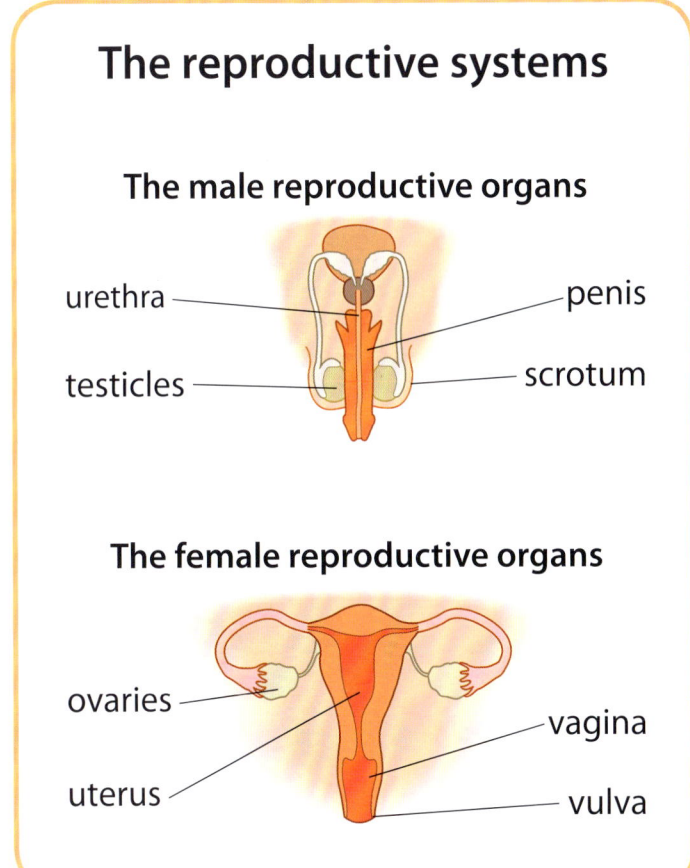

urethra

penis

testicles

scrotum

The female reproductive organs

ovaries

vagina

uterus

vulva

The respiratory system and the lungs

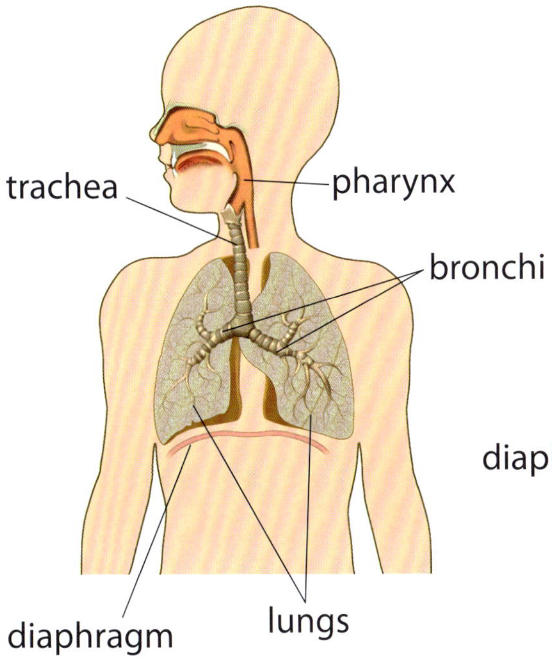

trachea

pharynx

bronchi

diaphragm

lungs

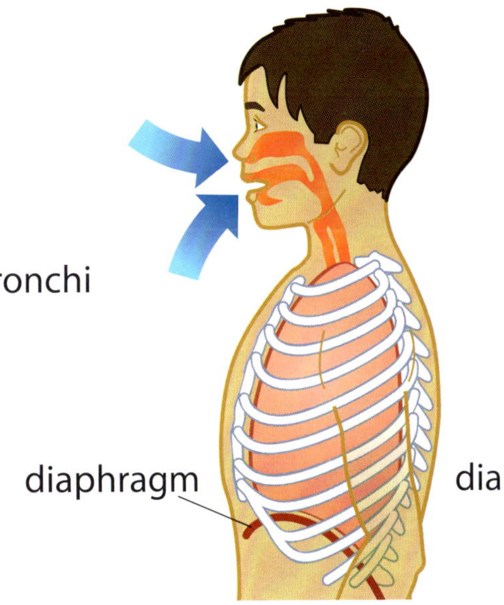

diaphragm

When we breathe in, the diaphragm contracts.

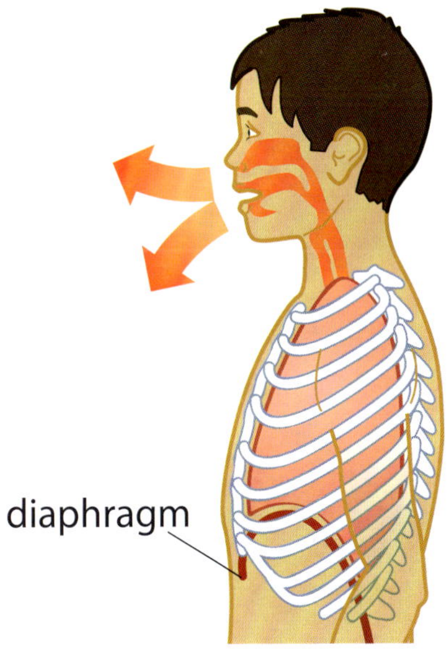

diaphragm

When we breathe out, the diaphragm relaxes.

Vertebrates

amphibian

bird

fish

mammal

reptile

Birds

All birds have a beak.

Birds that eat nuts and seeds have short beaks.

The eagle has a hooked beak for tearing meat.

Birds that catch fish have long, sharp beaks.

Birds that eat nectar from flowers have long, thin beaks.

Invertebrates

centipede

crab

insect

octopus

snail

spider

worm

Pollination and fertilisation

Pollen travels from the stamens to the
stigma by animal pollination.

Some plants use wind pollination
to reproduce.

The fertilised ovule becomes a seed.
A fruit forms around the seed.

The seed germinates.

Photosynthesis

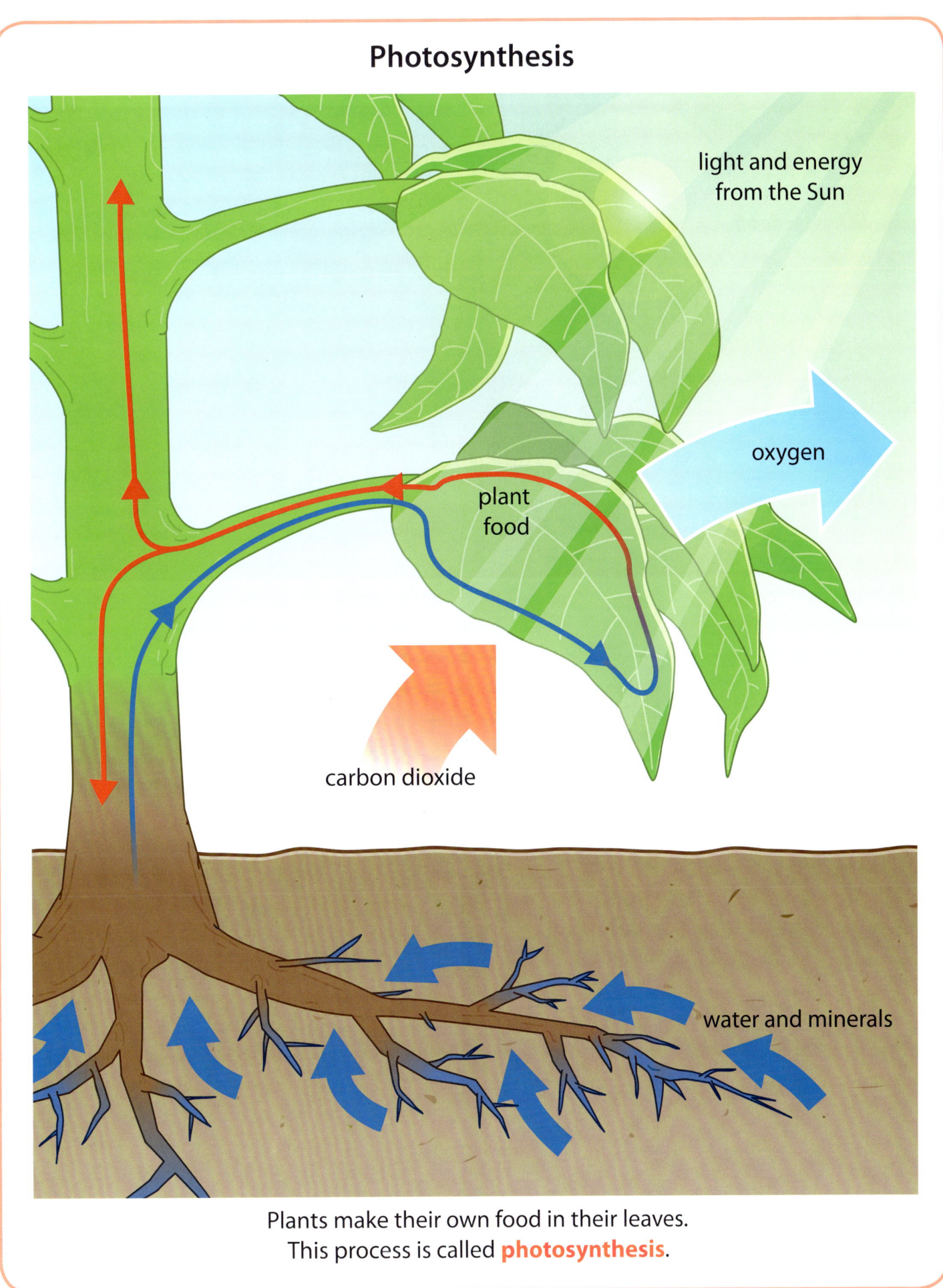

light and energy from the Sun

oxygen

plant food

carbon dioxide

water and minerals

Plants make their own food in their leaves.
This process is called **photosynthesis**.

Picture dictionary

The solar system

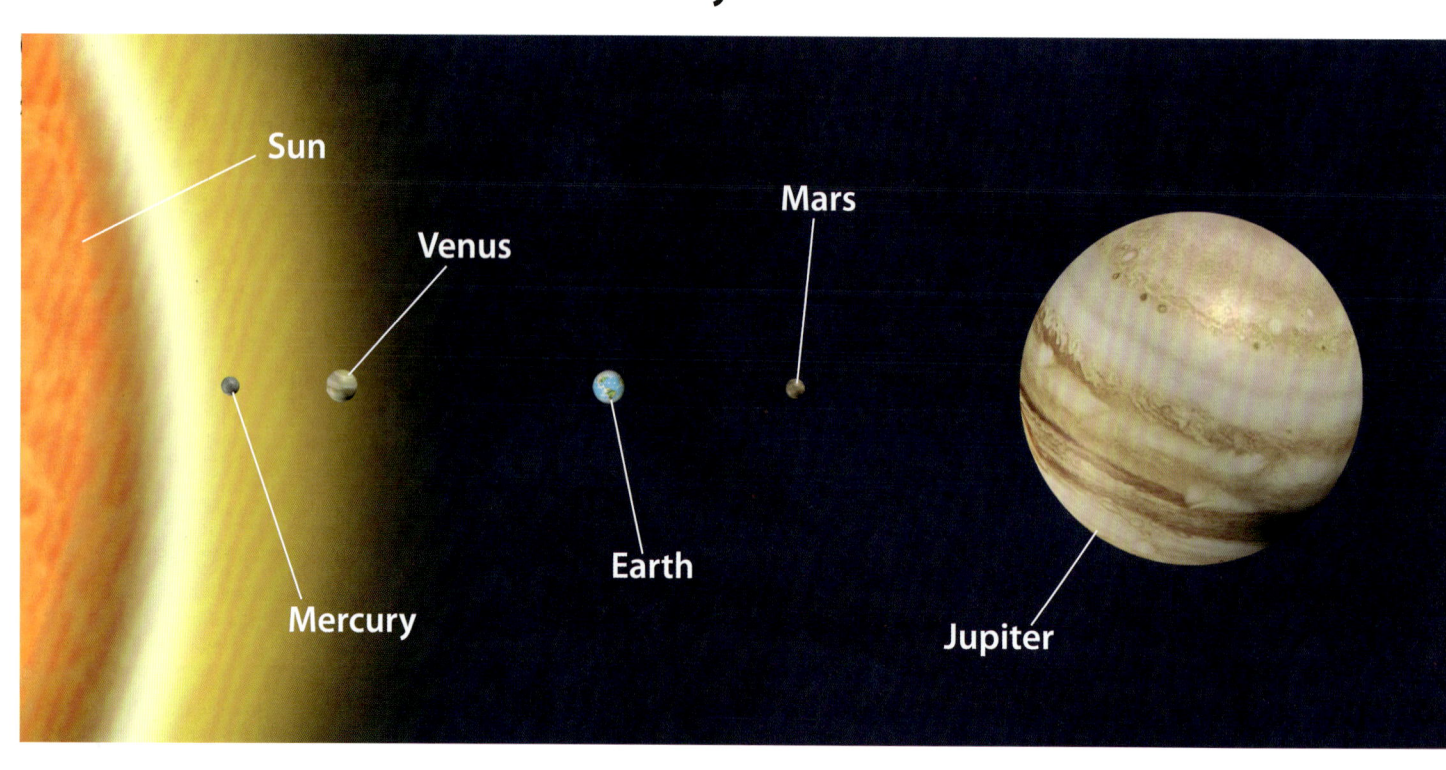

Sun

Venus

Mars

Mercury

Earth

Jupiter

Oceans and continents

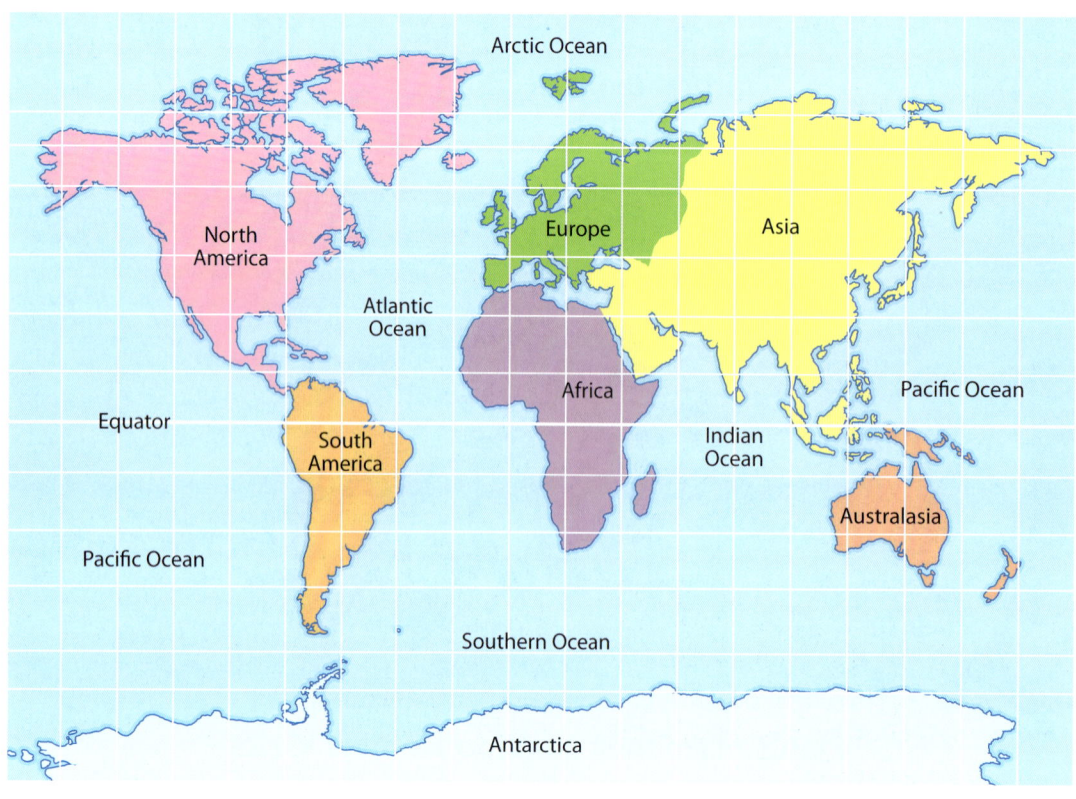

Arctic Ocean

North America

Europe

Asia

Atlantic Ocean

Africa

Pacific Ocean

Equator

South America

Indian Ocean

Australasia

Pacific Ocean

Southern Ocean

Antarctica

Lines of latitude and longitude

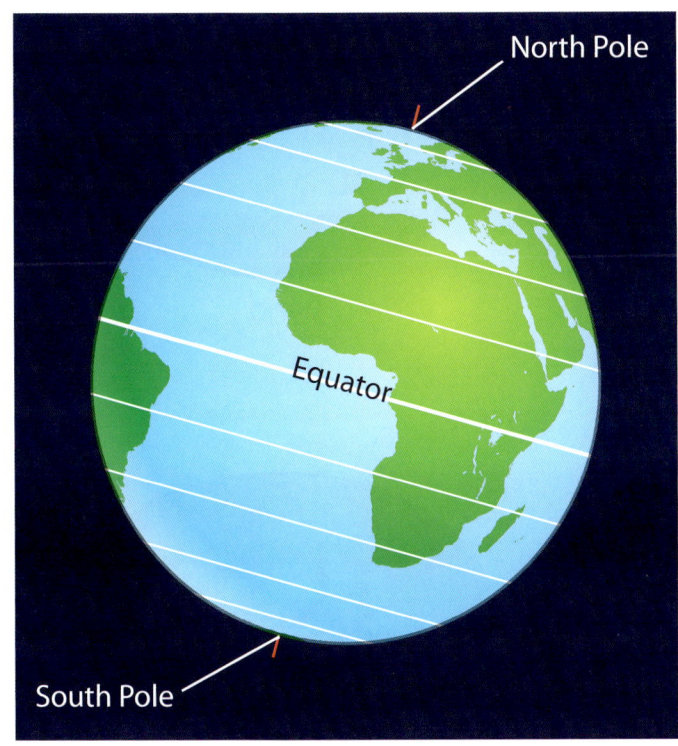

Lines of latitude

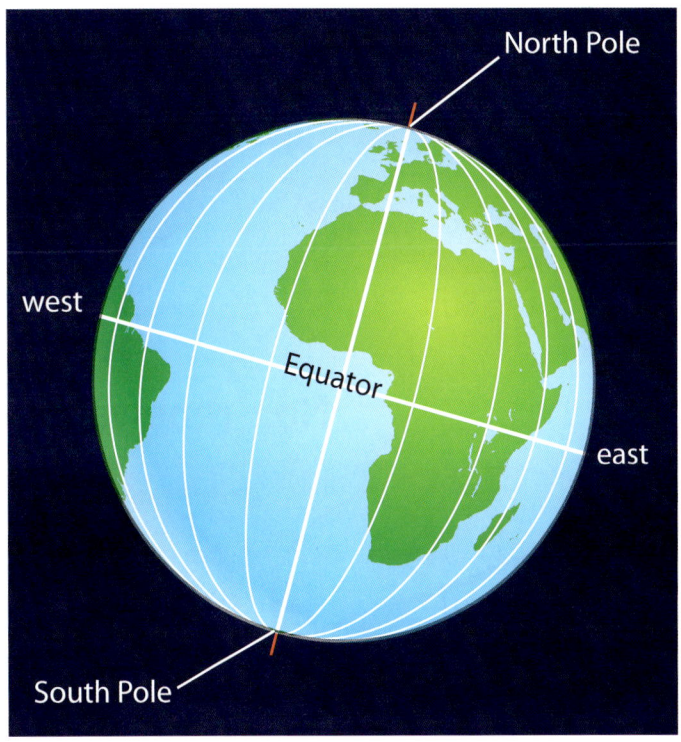

Lines of longitude

Forms of energy

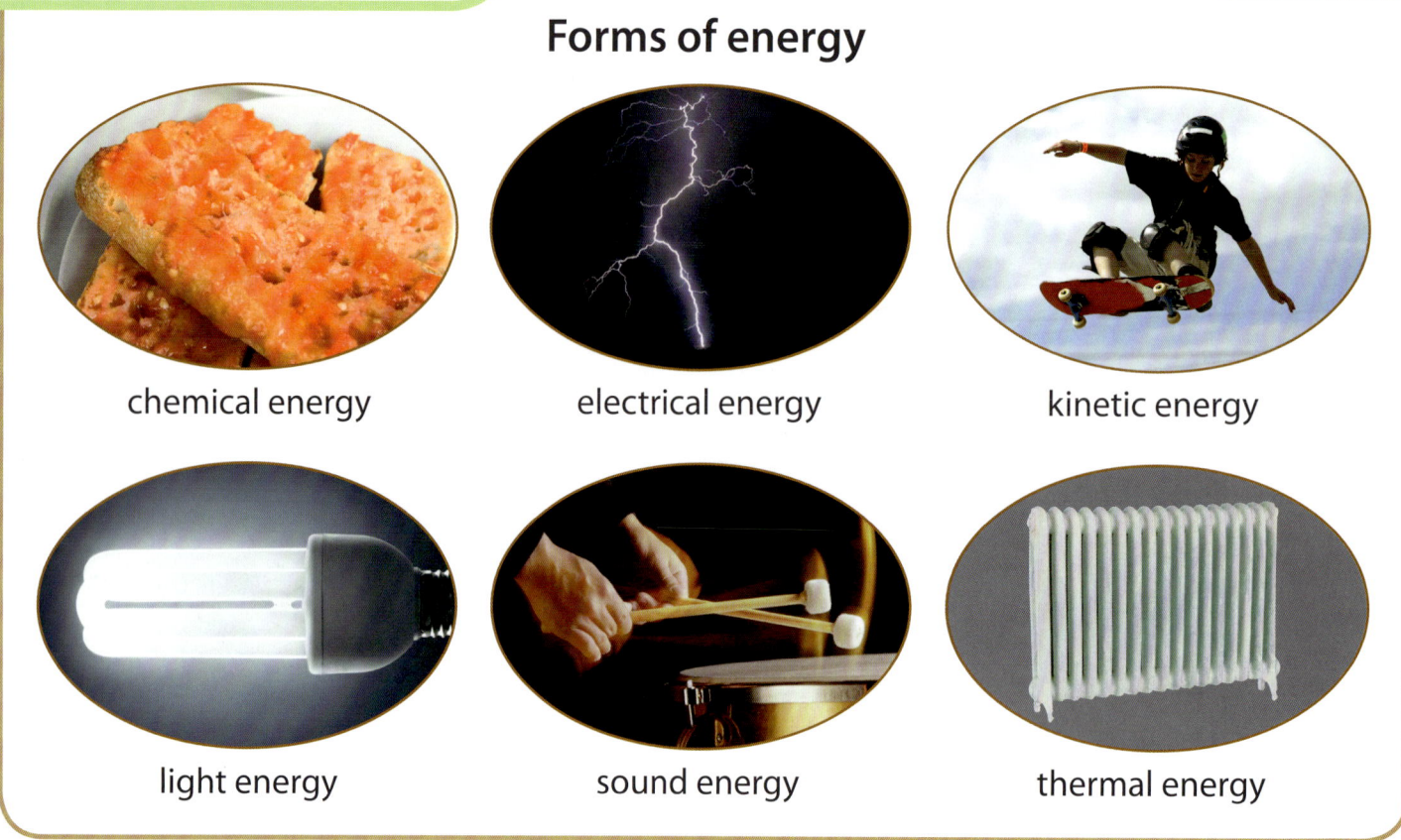

chemical energy

electrical energy

kinetic energy

light energy

sound energy

thermal energy

Renewable energy sources

the Sun

water

wind

Non-renewable energy sources

coal

gas

oil

Light

Light always travels in a straight line.

Light travels in all directions.

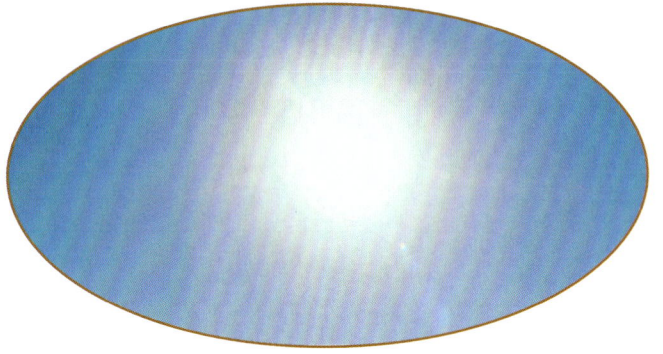

Light is the fastest form of energy.

The light from the Sun looks white, but it's made up of seven different colours.

Sound

Sound travels in all directions.

Sound can travel through solid objects.

Sound can travel through water.

When sound reflects off an object, we can hear an echo.

Simple machines

inclined plane

lever and fulcrum

pulley

screw

wedge

wheel and axle

Complex machines

bicycle

calculator

cooker

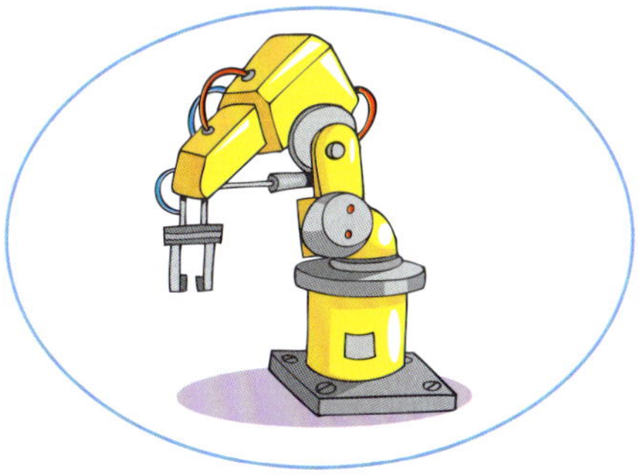

robot

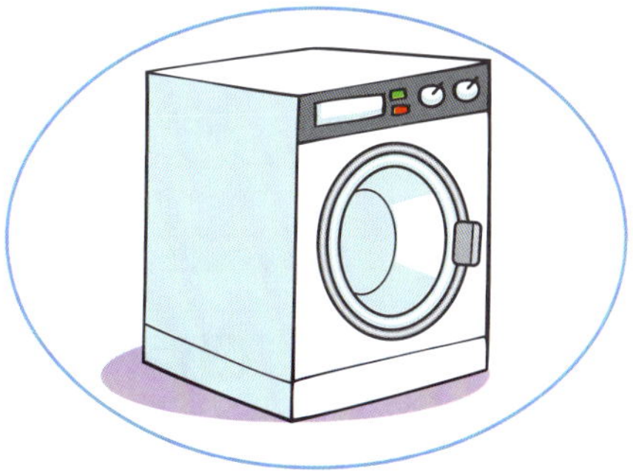

washing machine

How a complex machine works

brake lever

handlebars

gear controls

brakes

gears

pedal

tyre

front wheel

back wheel

The three states of matter

Solids have a definite shape and a definite volume.

Liquids don't have a definite shape, but they have a definite volume.

Gases don't have a definite shape and they don't have a definite volume.

Changes in matter

Physical changes

A physical change is when matter changes shape and state.

Chemical changes

A chemical change is when a new substance is produced.

Mixtures

Heterogeneous mixtures

In a heterogeneous mixture it's easy to see the different substances.

Homogeneous mixtures

In a homogeneous mixture it isn't possible to see the different substances.

Properties of materials

elastic

flexible

fragile

heat conductor

heat insulator

opaque   transparent

resistant

rigid

waterproof

The school community

Teaching staff

deputy head | head teacher | secretary | teachers

Non-teaching staff

caretaker | cleaners | cooks | supervisor

Local services

education services | social services | town planning services | health services

environmental services | water services | sports services | cultural services

Emergency services

fire brigade

medical services

police

Provinces

Guipúzcoa
A Coruña
Lugo
Asturias
Cantabria
Vizcaya
Álava
Navarra
Pontevedra
León
Burgos
La Rioja
Huesca
Lleida
Girona
Ourense
Zamora
Palencia
Valladolid
Soria
Zaragoza
Barcelona
Segovia
Tarragona
Salamanca
Ávila
Guadalajara
Teruel
Madrid
Cáceres
Toledo
Cuenca
Castellón
Valencia
Las Islas Baleares
Badajoz
Ciudad Real
Albacete
Alicante
Córdoba
Jaén
Murcia
Huelva
Sevilla
Granada
Almería
Cádiz
Málaga

Las Islas Canarias
Santa Cruz de Tenerife
Las Palmas
Ceuta
Melilla

Autonomous Communities

CANTABRIA
PAÍS VASCO
GALICIA
ASTURIAS
NAVARRA
LA RIOJA
CATALUÑA
CASTILLA - LEÓN
ARAGÓN
MADRID
EXTREMADURA
CASTILLA-LA MANCHA
VALENCIA
LAS ISLAS BALEARES
MURCIA
ANDALUCÍA

LAS ISLAS CANARIAS
Ceuta
Melilla

167

Rights

We can all vote and elect leaders.

We all have the right to have a job.

We all have access to public services, including education.

We are all protected by laws.

Responsibilities

We must respect public services.

We must respect each other's cultures, religions and political beliefs.

We must pay taxes to help pay for public services.

We must respect the law.

child population

adult population

elderly population

urban population

rural population

active population

inactive population

Population changes

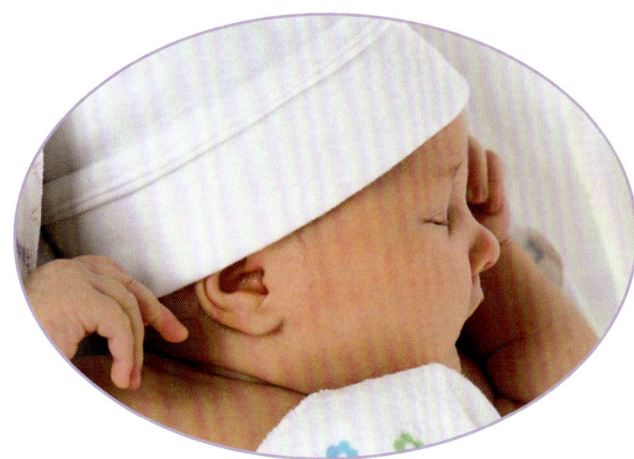

When **babies are born** the population increases. When **people die** the population decreases.

When **immigrants** come to our country the population increases. When **emigrants** leave our country the population decreases.

Prehistory

Palaeolithic period

Neolithic period

Ancient history

One of the most important civilisations in Ancient history was the Roman civilisation.

The Romans built outdoor theatres called **amphitheatres**.

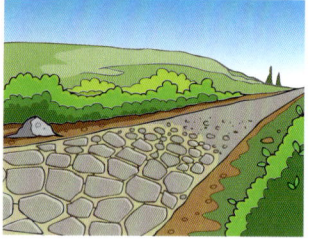

The Romans built **stone roads** to connect cities.

The Romans built **bridges** over rivers.

The Romans built **aqueducts** to carry water from rivers and lakes to cities.

The Middle Ages

During this period, two civilisations lived in the Iberian Peninsula: the Christian civilisation and the Islamic civilisation.

The Christian civilisation built religious buildings, such as **churches** and **cathedrals**.

The Islamic civilisation built religious buildings, such as **mosques**.

The Middle Ages

During this period, there were four groups of Christians:

nobles   clergy   craftsmen and merchants   peasants

The Modern Age

This period was a time of **discovery** and **scientific invention**.

Inventions such as the **compass** and more **accurate maps** meant that people could discover new lands.

An important invention of the Modern Age was the **printing press**.

The Contemporary Age

This period was a time of **industry** and **changes in society**.

  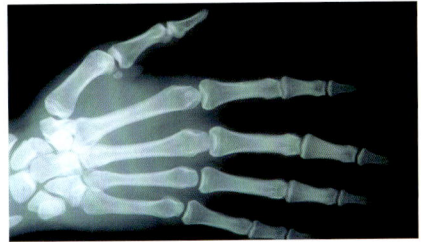

The steam engine made work quicker and easier.

People moved to towns and cities for work and urban populations increased.

There were important scientific inventions, such as the **x-ray**.

Macmillan Education
4 Crinan Street
London N1 9XW
A division of Macmillan Publishers Limited
Companies and representatives throughout the world

ISBN 978 0 230 72023 7

Written by Helen Sanderson
Designed by Anthony Godber
Illustrated by Ángeles Peinador, Mark Ruffle, Laszlo Veres, Ian Escott, Anthony Rule, Kathy Baxendale and Oxford Designers and Illustrators
Cover design by Mark Slader
Cover illustration by Elmentcius Koronel
Course consultant: Rocío Gutiérrez Burgos
Science consultant: Graham Peacock
Picture research by Zoe Spilberg
Recordings produced by James Richardson
Songs composed and arranged by Mark Fishlock

Author's acknowledgements
I would like to thank the staff at Macmillan for being so helpful and such good advisors at all times throughout this project. I am also very grateful to my patient mother for her support and suggestions during the writing process and to my father for his advice on scientific matters. And finally a big thank you to my husband and children for making it possible for me to work on this very enjoyable project at home.

Acknowledgements
The author and publishers would like to thank the following teachers and schools: Almudena Ibeas Jiménez, Colegio. Nuestra Señora de las Nieves, Madrid; Aránzazu Sánchez Rodríguez, C.P. Rosa de Luxemburgo, Aravaca, Madrid; Carlos Pérez Guillén, C.E.I.P. Dionisio Ridruejo, Madrid; Carmen Marcos Salazar, C.E.I.P. Ciudad de Columbia, Tres Cantos, Madrid; Catherine M. Anner, Colegio Internacional Alminar, Dos Hermanas, Sevilla; Celia Ojeda Esnoz, Colegio Alameda de Osuna, Madrid; Dionisio Jesús Montoya Lozano, Colegio Saladares –Grupo Attendis–, Roquetas de Mar, Almería; Eduardo Obeso Ceballos, C.P. Rosa de Luxemburgo, Aravaca, Madrid; Eider Goikouría Basterretxea, Colegio Jesús María, Bilbao, Vizcaya; Esther Ninou Rodríguez, Escola Sant Gervasi, Mollet del Vallès, Barcelona; Estíbaliz Medina Martín, C.P. Virgen de Navalazarza, San Agustín de Guadalix, Madrid; Eva Ampuero López, C.E.I.P. Emilio Casado, Alcobendas, Madrid; Francisca García Fraile, C.E.I.P. Fontarrón, Madrid; Gema Mena Blasco, C.E.I.P. Infanta Elena, Pozuelo de Alarcón, Madrid; Jairo Dopazo Alonso, Colegio Bilingüe Vallmont, Villanueva de la Cañada, Madrid; Janine Grant, Colegio Highlands, Sevilla; José Enrique Porras Ogalla, C.E.I.P. El Encinar, Torrelodones, Madrid; Laura Arroyo Campos, C.E.I.P. Ciudad de Columbia, Tres Cantos, Madrid; Laura Benítez Coloma, Institució La Miranda, Sant Just Desvern, Barcelona; María Cantó Collado, Colegio Bilingüe Vallmont, Villanueva de la Cañada, Madrid; Paloma González Megido, C.P. Marqués de Santillana, Palencia; Paula López Cabello, C.E.I.P. Gonzalo Fernández Córdoba, Madrid; Pilar Velasco García, C.P. Marqués de Santillana, Palencia; Roser Cantón Riera, Col·legi Marinada, Palau Solita i Plegamans, Barcelona; Sandra Rodríguez Figueroa, Colegio Internacional Alminar, Dos Hermanas, Sevilla; Sergio González Cenalmor, C.E.I.P. Vicente Aleixandre, Alcorcón, Madrid; Silvia San José Paul, C.E.I.P. El Cantizal, Las Rozas, Madrid; Susan Dreguer, Barcelona; Usoa García Hernández, Colegio Nuestra Señora de Europa, Getxo, Vizcaya; Zuriñe Sánchez, Colegio Sagrado Corazón Carmelitas, Vitoria-Gasteiz, Álava.

The publishers would like to thank Anthony Godber for his design expertise and invaluable input.

The authors and publishers would like to thank the following for permission to reproduce their photographic material:

Cover images by Paul Bricknell
Alamy/AA World Travel Library pp132, 171(br), Alamy/amana images inc pp15(background), 27(background), 39(background), 63(background), 75(background), 87(background), 113(background), Alamy/Andia pp140(tr), 172(bl), Alamy/Peter Arnold p39(l), 142(b), 154(tl), 173(br), Alamy/Krys Bailey p42(tl), Alamy/Roger Bamber p74, Alamy/Peter Barritt p120(br), Alamy/Juniors Bildarchiv p31(cb), Alamy/Blend Images pp19(br), 25, 152(bl), Alamy/blickwinkel pp4(whale), 34(br), 43(bl), 155(tcr), Alamy/Paul Broadbent pp117(br), 169(br), Alamy/Nigel Cattlin pp44(br), 156(br), Alamy/John Clemmer pp19(tr), 152(br), Alamy/Derek Croucher pp34(tr), 155(tr), Alamy/Eyecandy Images pp18(b), 152(c), Alamy/First Light p36(tr), Alamy/Xavier Fores-Joana Roncero p5(cb), Alamy/Kevin Foy p111(l), Alamy/Chris Gomersall p5(ct), Alamy/Juergen Henkelmann Photography p5(br), Alamy/L Heusinkveld p38, Alamy/D. Hurst pp16(tcl fish,chicken), 150(tr fish,chicken), Alamy/John Warburton-Lee Photography p63(c), Alamy/Caroline Jones p113(r), Alamy/Manor Photography p5(cr), Alamy/Mary Evans Picture Library pp141(br), 173(cr), Alamy/Mode Images Ltd p96(tr), Alamy/Keith Morris p105(c), Alamy/nagelestock.com pp127(tl), 134(cl), 171(tl), Alamy/Richard Naude pp117(tl), 124(r), 169(tl), Alamy/PhotoAlto pp75(br), 160(chemical energy), Alamy/Picturebank p13, Alamy/Picture Contact BV pp117(tr), 169(tr), Alamy/Pictorial Press Ltd p143(cl), Alamy/Denys Prokofyev p6(tr), Alamy/Digifoto Sapphire pp92(bl), 164(cr), Alamy/Malcolm Schuyl p31(ct), Alamy/Superclic p37(6), Alamy/Peter Titmuss p113(cr), Alamy/Andrew Twort pp16(tcl meat), 150(tr meat), Alamy/Genevieve Vallee pp32(bl), 154(bcl), Alamy/Wildlife GmBH p37(10); **Bananastock** pp4(tl), 18(t), 67(l), 152(tr); **Brand X** pp32(br), 33(t), 37(3), 40(ct), 52(cb), 60(tl), 75(ct), 122, 154(bl, tr), 160(kinetic energy, br); **ComStock Images** pp6(bl, br), 7(bl, cr), 75(tr), 87(tl), 160(thermal energy), 171(bl); **Corbis** pp19(l), 31(t), 40(tr), 42(bl), 60(tr), 128, 134(tr), 152(tl), 171(cr), Corbis/Eloy Alonso p107(c), 166(c), Corbis/Bevis Boobacca p69(tr), Corbis/Emely p5(bl), Corbis/Glowimages pp16(ct), 150(ct), Corbis/Chinch Gryniewicz;Ecoscene p73(tl), Corbis/Don Hammond/Design Pics p4(bl), Corbis/Rune Hellestad p24(br), Corbis/Imagemore Co Ltd pp16(bcr), 150(bcl), Corbis/Dennis Johnson; Papilio p32(tr), Corbis/Matthias Kulka pp24(tl), 75(cb), 87(c), Corbis/Sarah Monte/Westend 61 p27(tl), Corbis/Moodboard pp75(bl), 160(light energy), Corbis/Ocean pp35(tl), 67(r),105(t), 116(bl), 124(l), 168(bl), Corbis/Tim Pannell p30(bl), Corbis/Parke John/Visuals Unlimited p33(c), Corbis/Arthur W.V. Mace; Milepost 92 ½, Corbis/Sergio Pitamitz p144, Corbis/Monty Rakusen/ cultura p48, Corbis/Galen Rowell p45, Corbis/Steve Sparrow/cultura p5(tr), Corbis/Wolfram Steinberg p73(b), Corbis/The Art Archive p136(tl), Corbis/The Gallery Collection p136(tr), Corbis/Visuals Unlimited pp24(cl), 52(t), Corbis/Granger Wootz/Blend Images pp116(tr), 168(tr), Corbis/Ed Young/ AgStock Images pp16(tl), 150(tl); **Creatas** p145(l); **Digital Vision** pp4(snail), 30(tl), 34(tl), 35(bl, cb, cl, snail), 36(br), 37(8, 9), 39(r), 40(cb, bl, tl, br), 44(tl,), 51(l), 52(b), 155(tl, bl), 156(tl, bl); **Fotolibra** pp16(bl), 150(bl), Fotolibra/Bob Crook p8, Fotolibra/June Egglestone p75(tl), Fotolibra/Mark Ferguson p84(bcl, bcr), Fotolibra/James W Fowler p101(tcl), Fotolibra/Martyn Franklin pp69(br), 84(bl, bc. br), 161(br), Fotolibra/Maria Galan Food pp7(tl), 113(cl), 120(tr), Fotolibra/Len Sparrow pp16(bcl), 141(tr), 150(cbr), 173(cl), Fotolibra/Cherry D Spooner pp140(tl), 173(tl), Fotolibra/Rob Wyatt pp136(br), 148(b); **Fundación Joaquín Díaz,Urueña, Spain** p111(cr); **Getty**/pp 6(c, tl, cb), 7(br, tr), 16(tr), 32(bcl), 36(cr), 37(1, 4, 7), 42(br), 43(tl), 44(bl inset) 49(b), 56(t), 60(bl), 73(d), 87(cr, cb), 92(tr), 107(l), 113(l), 118(t), 123(l), 127(br), 130, 134(tl), 136(bl), 139, 142(c), 143(l, cr, r), 148(ct), 150(ctr), 154(bcr), 156(bl inset), 160(br,bc,water), 166(l), 171(cl), 173(bc), Getty/Neil Bromhall p24(cr), Getty/Kryssia Campos pp32(bcr), 154(br), Getty/Danita Delimont pp140(cr), 173(tcl), Getty/Rebecca Emery p26, Getty/English School pp140(br), 173(tr), Getty/Yasuhide Fumoto p67(c), Getty/Fuse p12, Getty/Gyro Photography/amanaimages RF pp44(tr), 156(tr), Getty/Gerald Hinde pp36(bl), 154(reptile), Getty/Nossa Productions p27(bl), Getty/Max Oppenheim p23(l), Getty/Richard Passmore p63(l), Getty/Richard Price p160(sound energy), Getty/Michael Rosenfeld pp16(tcr), 150(tcl), Getty/Bernard Roussel p87(bl), Getty/James Smith pp69(tl), 161(tl), Getty/Steve Smith p160(tr), Getty/Stephen Swain Photography

Printed and bound in China

2018   2017   2016   2015   2014
15 14 13 12 11 10 9 8 7 6